Self Esteem

Self Esteem

Gael Lindenfield

Thorsons
An Imprint of HarperCollins*Publishers*

To my little brother John,
whom I now look up to with much love and admiration.

Thorsons
An Imprint of HarperCollins*Publishers*
77–85 Fulham Palace Road,
Hammersmith, London W6 8JB
1160 Battery Street,
San Francisco, California 94111–1213

Published by Thorsons 1995
11 13 15 17 19 20 18 16 14 12

© Gael Lindenfield 1995

Gael Lindenfield asserts the moral right
to be identified as the author of this work

A catalogue record for this book
is available from the British Library

ISBN 0 7225 3017 X

Printed in Great Britain by
Caledonian International Book Manufacturing Ltd, Glasgow

Contents

Acknowledgements

Many thanks again to all the many participants on my courses who have shared so honestly and worked so courageously to rebuild their damaged self esteem.

Thanks also to James and Marie for sharing some of their enviable knowledge about cars.

Thanks to Ari Badaines for unknowingly sowing one of the seeds which led to the development of my thinking around this subject and also for being such an inspirational and creative psychodrama trainer. I would also add that he deserves considerable credit for helping me to rescue my own flagging self esteem on several crucial occasions.

Thanks yet again to Jessica Stockham for her amazing illustrations. I feel very privileged to have such a creative and humorous colleague whom I can depend on to understand what I want without my even realizing what that is!

Many, many thanks to my family (and Marie) for tolerating the tension and feeding me during the final fraught stages of producing this book.

Finally, as ever, my husband Stuart has been a wonderful support. Not only does he willingly give up his increasingly precious free time to edit on demand but he also acts as a stimulating sounding board for my ideas even when they emerge at the most inconvenient times!

Introduction

Low self esteem is no longer just a problem of the deprived, depressed and depraved. Even the most confident, caring and successful among us are finding it harder and harder to feel consistently 'good-enough'. It's a hard uphill struggle to feel OK about ourselves when we are confronted not only with challenging work appraisals but also with a rapidly increasing number of books and TV programmes on how to be a better father, mother, son, daughter, lover, friend and neighbour as well!

In the last few decades, popular psychology and the mass media have done wonders for our self-awareness and given us some exciting and challenging self-development goals, but they have also strained the limits of many people's self esteem. And I am assured by my own reading and by the experience of colleagues in other countries that the problem is international. All over the world, masses of people are beginning collectively to stagger under a mound of self-destructive guilt. At the same time as we look in our mirrors and judge ourselves to be too fat, too thin, too old, too young, too poor, too lazy, too uneducated, we may also berate ourselves for even caring about such selfish irrelevancies in the full knowledge of the life-threatening famines and wars that we now know only too well others are suffering.

Whom Will This Book Help?

So it seems that, in the unhelpful context of a confidence-shattering recession, the new caring values of the well-informed 1990s are setting us even more unachievable standards. As a result, millions of people who previously have never questioned their worth are now turning to the world of therapy to boost their self-respect. I firmly believe that for many people who, like myself, have had their self esteem deeply damaged in childhood, or who have experienced a major trauma in adulthood, professional counselling should be freely available. Such people both need and deserve more help than a short book can hope to offer them. But equally, I know that there are many other people who perhaps are not in such severe emotional pain and distress, who could make very effective use of some DIY self esteem boosting materials. So in writing this book I primarily had in mind the needs of people:

- who generally have enough confidence and self-worth to enable them to 'get by' but suspect (quite rightly) that they will get very much more out of themselves and their lives if their self esteem levels were *more consistently high*
- whose self esteem is going through a *temporary bad patch* (e.g. perhaps partly due to a failed exam, a romantic rejection, divorce, redundancy, change of job or family responsibility) and who are therefore looking for a way of making a speedy and effective recovery
- who are wanting to improve their ability to enhance and *build the self esteem of others*.

I hope that the book will also help those who may be waiting in the queue for professional help, or who may want to supplement their counselling with a self-help boost.

How This Book First Came into Being

Isn't it strange how some simple casual conversations can have a profound effect on the course of our lives? I certainly can trace the original trigger to writing this book back to a lighthearted five-minute chat that took place about 10 years ago between myself and one of my trainers, Ari Badaines. (At the time I know that neither of us was in 'profound-thinking mode', as I recall our attention was much more focused on filling our empty stomachs!)

Unfortunately, as Ari now works on the other side of the globe, we only bump into each other every few years. When we did so again recently I found it interesting that he too could remember in detail the piece of apparently insignificant small talk we made en route to the canteen. Our conversation went something like this:

Ari: How's it going? What are you doing these days?

Gael: I've recently set up a mental health project and we've established a whole range of different self-help groups for people struggling to cope on their own with a wide variety of problems such as depression, phobias, anxiety, obsession, eating problems, lack of assertiveness, parenting, and caring for the elderly at home.

Ari: How are they working out?

Gael: Well, they're very popular. People certainly enjoy being with others who are experiencing the same difficulties – but I'm not sure the groups are 'curing' anyone. It's interesting because I find the very same problems coming up again and again in each of them.

Ari: I know what you mean. I think I am coming to the conclusion that there is only *one* problem – and it's one that almost every one shares: LOW SELF ESTEEM.

Soon after that conversation I decided to experiment with bringing people from some of the different groups together under the nondescript title 'The Tuesday Group'. This move proved to be remarkably successful. Because we could no longer keep the focus on symptoms (they were too diverse), we had to focus on everyone's shared root problem – lack of confidence. This unexpected turn of events set me thinking and experimenting yet again! As a result, the next decade of both my personal and professional life has been dominated by my quest to discover the secrets of self-confidence. With this book I feel that I may well be near the gates of my destination! (Are you smiling, Ari?)

A Luxury or a Necessity?

Self esteem, I have discovered, is not only the golden key which unlocks our potential to become Super-confident, it also acts as the *heart* of our psychological selves and is just as critical to our survival as its physical counterpart. When it is strong and healthy and it is pumping personal power through our emotional veins, we have the vitality and motivation to take on the world as our 'oyster'. But when it is struggling, strained and lifeless, so are we!

But isn't this all self-deluding escapist psychobabble, the cynics ask? What the world and the individuals in it need today is not selfish soul-searching, but some effective political and economic strategies. This used to be a common argument, but now thank goodness there is plenty of erudite research flowing out from universities all over the world which is supporting the less scientifically based musings of therapists like myself. Even a few cost-cutting governments (including those of the US and Russia) are now seeing the sense of allocating resources to self esteem building projects as the evidence mounts that high self esteem is not only the life-blood of happy healthy individuals, but also of well-functioning groups, organizations *and* communities.

An Overview of the Book

Like my earlier personal development books, this one is also designed as a self-help programme. It can be done on your own or in the more supportive setting of a group.

There are four main sections of the book, each covering a different area:

Section One (Exploring the Essential Elements) explains the concept and effects of self esteem and how it is built, boosted – and battered.

Section Two (Laying the Foundations for Action) describes the essential healing and self-protective strategies needed to underpin self esteem building work.

Section Three (Self-help Programmes) offers practical programmes of exercises and checklists to help you rebuild flagging self-worth and keep it in tip-top condition. It includes an exercise programme which can be used as an annual 'service' for your self esteem, and another which will help you to regain personal power after an emotional trauma such as a rejection, bereavement, divorce or redundancy, or a major mistake, setback or failure.

Section Four (Using Your Strength to Empower) contains tips and exercises to help you develop your ability to build self esteem in others. It includes guidelines on how to do this in the three specific roles of Manager, Parent and Citizen.

You will probably derive most benefit from the book if you first read it through reasonably quickly to get an overall idea of the material and practical work it contains. You will then be better able to plan an effective programme for yourself or your group, using the book's different sections to suit your individual needs.

I hope you find this self esteem building work as fascinating and rewarding as I and many hundreds of others have done. Good luck!

Section 1
Exploring the Essential Elements

1

What Is Self Esteem?

In my search for the perfect definition of self esteem, I have found literally hundreds of different views and descriptions. My head began to reel as I tried to face the task of summarizing all these in a couple of neat paragraphs. Perhaps largely to protect my own mental health, I therefore decided to do something different!

I thought that I would start from the perspective of my own personal experience. After all, as I indicated in the Introduction, I have much more than an academic interest in this subject. Self esteem building is still very much part of my own personal as well as professional life.

When I began to reflect on my own experience, I began to think that one of the reasons why there are so many variations in the definition of self esteem is that it is essentially a 'state of being'. It is a dynamic, subjective event in our bodies and our minds rather than any static, tangible 'thing' that can be directly and easily observed and measured. To make the scene even more complicated, it seems that when we experience our self esteem, a whole chain of mini-happenings take place. Sometimes it seems these can *all* take place in the flash of an instant, but at other times they may slowly develop step by step over a much longer period of time.

The Inside Story

On the opposite page is a simple analysis of what happens in my mind and body when I feel a sense of good, sound self esteem (even though I may not be consciously aware of the process taking place).

I hope this description fits your own experience. If it doesn't I'd be interested sometime to hear what appears to be happening to you when you perceive your self esteem to be high. In the meantime, I hope you'll accept my subjective analysis as a working definition for the purposes of this book!

The Outside Story

Now let's look at this self esteem experience from the outer perspective, and examine how it is seen through other people's eyes.

As you read this next section, try to think of people you know who have some or all of these attributes. Having some visual examples in your mind of self esteem in action will help to strengthen your motivation to achieve your goal! Seeing certainly helps the believing, especially during some of the uphill steps in changing our psychological selves!

How We Can Recognize a Person with High Self Esteem

Here are some of the most significant qualities which we can commonly observe in the *appearance* and *behaviour* of people whose self esteem is consistently good.

- CALM and RELAXED – They appear to be at ease and in control, even when faced with difficult and daunting

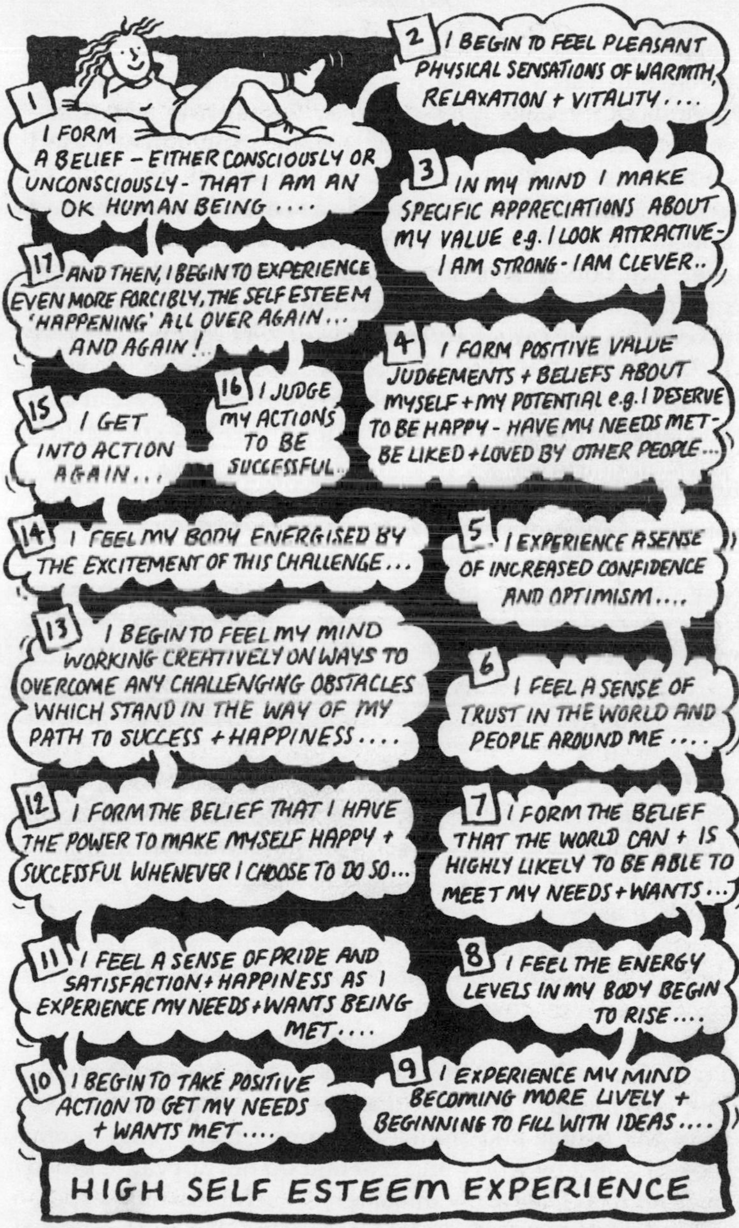
1 I FORM A BELIEF – EITHER CONSCIOUSLY OR UNCONSCIOUSLY – THAT I AM AN OK HUMAN BEING ....
2 I BEGIN TO FEEL PLEASANT PHYSICAL SENSATIONS OF WARMTH, RELAXATION + VITALITY ....
3 IN MY MIND I MAKE SPECIFIC APPRECIATIONS ABOUT MY VALUE e.g. I LOOK ATTRACTIVE – I AM STRONG – I AM CLEVER ..
4 I FORM POSITIVE VALUE JUDGEMENTS + BELIEFS ABOUT MYSELF + MY POTENTIAL e.g. I DESERVE TO BE HAPPY – HAVE MY NEEDS MET – BE LIKED + LOVED BY OTHER PEOPLE ...
5 I EXPERIENCE A SENSE OF INCREASED CONFIDENCE AND OPTIMISM ....
6 I FEEL A SENSE OF TRUST IN THE WORLD AND PEOPLE AROUND ME ....
7 I FORM THE BELIEF THAT THE WORLD CAN + IS HIGHLY LIKELY TO BE ABLE TO MEET MY NEEDS + WANTS ...
8 I FEEL THE ENERGY LEVELS IN MY BODY BEGIN TO RISE ....
9 I EXPERIENCE MY MIND BECOMING MORE LIVELY + BEGINNING TO FILL WITH IDEAS ....
10 I BEGIN TO TAKE POSITIVE ACTION TO GET MY NEEDS + WANTS MET ....
11 I FEEL A SENSE OF PRIDE AND SATISFACTION + HAPPINESS AS I EXPERIENCE MY NEEDS + WANTS BEING MET ....
12 I FORM THE BELIEF THAT I HAVE THE POWER TO MAKE MYSELF HAPPY + SUCCESSFUL WHENEVER I CHOOSE TO DO SO ...
13 I BEGIN TO FEEL MY MIND WORKING CREATIVELY ON WAYS TO OVERCOME ANY CHALLENGING OBSTACLES WHICH STAND IN THE WAY OF MY PATH TO SUCCESS + HAPPINESS ....
14 I FEEL MY BODY ENERGISED BY THE EXCITEMENT OF THIS CHALLENGE ...
15 I GET INTO ACTION AGAIN ...
16 I JUDGE MY ACTIONS TO BE SUCCESSFUL ..
17 AND THEN, I BEGIN TO EXPERIENCE EVEN MORE FORCIBLY, THE SELF ESTEEM 'HAPPENING' ALL OVER AGAIN ... AND AGAIN! ..
HIGH SELF ESTEEM EXPERIENCE

challenges. Their posture is usually upright and there is rarely much sign of tension in their faces or limbs and, after periods of increased pressure, they will always take 'time-out' to recover and quickly regain their serenity and composure.

- WELL-NURTURED – They exude a sense of well-being and appear fully 'at home' in their well-nourished and well-exercised bodies. It is obvious that they have taken care to groom and present themselves well even when they have chosen a very casual style of dress. They never routinely indulge in self-destructive eating, drinking or sleeping habits and they always give themselves extra physical care and attention when they are under stress or experiencing physical illness.

- ENERGETIC and PURPOSEFUL – They are full of life, both mentally and physically. They usually enjoy working and undertake whatever task they do with enthusiasm and enjoyment. They are highly motivated and, unless they are in a period of creative transition and change, always maintain a clear sense of direction. So, although they are careful to stop and recharge their batteries from time to time, you won't catch them aimlessly drifting or getting stuck in ruts.

- OPEN and EXPRESSIVE – They are WYSIWYG people (like the 'What You See Is What You Get' computer programmes!). They communicate in a direct, straightforward manner and (unless they are poets or politicians, of course!) they tend to speak plainly and use non-verbal gestures which clearly indicate what is going on for them emotionally. They are very capable of being spontaneous when they choose to be so, but they can summon up superb emotional control when they want their heads to rule their hearts.

- POSITIVE and OPTIMISTIC – From both the way they talk and act, you get the sense that they are expecting the best from the people and the world around them. They rarely look disabled by worry and fear and do not appear to brood over regrets. They view mistakes as useful learning experiences which are unlikely to be repeated. When they meet obstacles to their progress they openly and safely release their frustration and then return to solve the problem with increased vigour and determination.

You can often hear them talking about the future with excitement, and they view opportunities for change and development with genuine interest and enthusiasm.

- SELF-RELIANT – They are highly capable of acting independently and autonomously. They do not constantly seek the approval or opinion of others before making decisions or taking action. They enjoy their own company and would not necessarily need the fraternity or direction of others to help them relax or work efficiently. They take full responsibility for securing and overseeing their own financial stability. When they do decide to innovate or take risks, you can be sure they have prepared suitable contingency plans and will not take help from others for granted.

- SOCIABLE and CO-OPERATIVE – Even if they are naturally introverted by nature (unless they have a good reason not to be so), they are friendly and trusting of other people from any creed or culture. In meetings and social gatherings they do not hog more than their fair share of attention. It is obvious that they often seem just as interested in listening to others as they are in having their own voices heard. They can enjoy being a member of a partnership, a team or a community and are usually willing to compromise and negotiate to secure harmonious relationships and a good deal for the 'common good'. They are never threatened by the success and happiness of others, and so can often be seen actively encouraging other people's development and welfare. Although they often emerge as the natural leaders of groups, they are also able and willing to share power and authority and delegate appropriately.

- APPROPRIATELY ASSERTIVE – They stand up for their own needs and rights but, equally, they can be relied upon to fight for justice for others as well. If occasionally their assertive attempts to solve important problems fail, they are happy to use both passive or aggressive strategies to obtain fair and sensible resolutions.

- SELF-DEVELOPING – Although it is obvious that they have a deservedly high degree of self-worth, they are often self-reflective. They are happy to acknowledge their imperfections and mistakes as well as their strengths and achievements, because they are continually searching for ways and means to improve their behaviour and performance. Although they will not waste much energy or time doing battle with aggressive and destructive critics, they do welcome constructive feedback and advice. You can expect them to be engaged in some ongoing educational or personal development project (even though in our envious eyes they already appear to have reached the pinnacle of perfection!).

Don't be daunted by this idealized description of a self esteem paragon of virtue. Even if you were lucky enough to meet a person who displayed all of these characteristics all of the time, I think it is unlikely that you would feel diminished in his or her presence. Contrary to what many people (who mistakenly confuse high self esteem with arrogance) think, when we are in the company of people with very high self esteem we tend to feel better, not worse about ourselves. When we are with them we are likely to feel:

- AT EASE – Because they are often so relaxed and we sense that we have full permission to be ourselves. They will not need us to be something that we are not in order to make themselves feel superior or to impress anyone else who may be around.
- SAFE – Because they will never use bullying tactics to make themselves feel more in control. Our sense of security is enhanced because we know where we stand with them. We trust that they will give us honest and direct feedback and do not fear any rumblings under the carpet. Knowing that they have a strong survival instinct and are prepared to fight courageously when under threat, we willingly depend on them. We can rest assured that they will readily take the lead and assertively defend anyone's rights in the event of

injustice or abuse.

- VALUED – Because they tend to show appreciation for each individual's strengths, efforts and achievements. They do not demand that we are mirror images of them and will actively show respect for our views and values even though these may be very different from their own. Because they are so aware and accepting of their own shortcomings, they do not expect us to be perfect, so we feel can be both unconditionally liked and loved.
- STIMULATED – Because they are brilliant and inspiring role-models. Their energy and enthusiasm is highly infectious, so that being with them kindles potential in us that we may never have even dreamed we had. Indeed, in their presence we often feel our courage and motivation grow as our own self esteem is spontaneously rekindled and nourished.

So although high self esteem is essentially an *internal psychological event*, it also can exert a powerfully *beneficial effect on the external environment*. But of course (as most of us can testify from our own everyday uncomfortable experiences), the reverse is also unfortunately true. *People who have low self esteem not only consistently sabotage their own health, welfare and happiness, but they also frequently exert a depressing and sometimes highly detrimental effect on the world around them.*

Let's remind ourselves of the negative cycle of low self esteem attitudes and behaviour.

Why Do Some People Have More Self Esteem than Others?

I firmly believe that we all start off in life with the same *potential* for good self esteem. How many babies and young toddlers have you met who appear to be thinking negatively

1 I FORM A NEGATIVE BELIEF IN MYSELF THAT I AM NOT AN OK HUMAN BEING...
2 I BEGIN TO FEEL SENSATIONS OF COLDNESS, HEAVINESS + TENSION IN MY BODY...
3 I HAVE DEVALUING THOUGHTS ABOUT MYSELF e.g. I AM UNLOVABLE - I AM UNWORTHY OF SUCCESS - I AM STUPID, etc.....
4 I BEGIN TO EXPERIENCE A LOSS OF SELF-CONFIDENCE + FEEL PESSIMISTIC..
5 I FIND THAT I AM LOSING TRUST IN PEOPLE + THE WORLD AROUND ME.....
6 I FORM THE BELIEF THAT IT IS UNLIKELY THAT THE WORLD WILL EVER BE ABLE TO MEET MY NEEDS OR GIVE ME HAPPINESS...
7 I STOP BOTHERING TO TRY TO GET MY NEEDS MET OR ACHIEVE SUCCESS...
8 I BECOME AWARE THAT I AM ACTUALLY MUCH LESS HAPPY + SUCCESSFUL THAN SOME OTHER PEOPLE AROUND ME....
9 I ALLOW OTHER PEOPLE WHO I PERCEIVE AS MORE POWERFUL TO TAKE ADVANTAGE OF ME...
10 I BEGIN TO SILENTLY RESENT OTHERS WHO ARE MORE SUCCESSFUL + POWERFUL AND WISH THEM ILL...
11 I JUDGE MYSELF TO BE A 'NASTY' PERSON FOR HAVING SUCH THOUGHTS...
12 I BEGIN TO BEHAVE IN WAYS WHICH ARE SELF-PUNITIVE AND SELF-DESTRUCTIVE eg. SACRIFICING MYSELF TO OTHERS IN AN ATTEMPT TO GAIN THEIR ESTEEM...
13 I LOOK IN THE MIRROR + SEE THE RESULTS OF CONTINUALLY ABUSING MYSELF + BEING ABUSED BY OTHERS...
14 I REINFORCE MY BELIEF THAT I AM NOT AN OK HUMAN BEING...
15 THEN - I BEGIN TO EXPERIENCE THE LOW SELF ESTEEM CYCLE ALL OVER AGAIN...
LOW SELF ESTEEM CYCLE

about themselves?! Unfortunately, we all know how quickly the picture soon changes. By the time children are ready for school, the differences between each one's self esteem are noticeably marked.

It would appear that the seeds of our self esteem begin to grow and develop as soon as we begin to experience a sense of ourselves as individuals. Typically it then embarks on a roller-coaster ride, being cultivated and strengthened one day only to be knocked back and diminished the next. The kind of childhood we experience is particularly important, because it is then that our basic personality traits and habits are formed.

Let's look for a moment at some of the ways children's natural propensity to feel good about being themselves may be threatened in the course of *everyday life*. I have listed below some examples which I have either experienced personally or have heard related to me. As you are reading you could make a note of any of your own special memories as this could be useful to refer to when you begin to do the practical work in later sections.

WHAT DECREASES CHILDREN'S SELF ESTEEM?

- **not having their basic needs adequately met** – especially when they notice that others may be receiving much better love, care and sustenance (e.g. younger brothers and sisters are getting more attention, or different races and classes are receiving privileges and a high standard of living while they are deprived of their basic right to adequate food and shelter)
- **having their feelings persistently ignored or denied** (e.g. a parent not responding to a cry for help or noticing the look of joy or worry on their faces – or saying, *'You **shouldn't** be sad about that, it's only.....you ought to be **excited**'*)
- **being put-down, ridiculed or humiliated** – especially for just being their genetically inherited natural selves or being a certain age (e.g. *'You're just a baby still'; 'You boys always...'; 'You've never been very good with figures – even in your pram*

you refused to count the beads' or 'You're just like your Grandfather, headstrong and stubborn')

- **being required to assume a 'false-self' in order to impress others or get their needs met** – especially if they are continually given the impression that this requirement is not so much to do with manners or protocol but is necessary because their 'real self' isn't good-enough (e.g. *'When you're at school make sure you don't say or do.....like you usually do'* or *'You can't go out looking like that, it shows up your.....what do you think people are going to think?'* – or when a lively enquiring child is told *'If you ask me why one more time I'll stop the car and you'll have to walk home'*)

- **being forced to engage in unsuitable activities** – especially if there is a high chance that they will not do them well because they have little aptitude or motivation (e.g. forcing a tone-deaf child to play the violin, or insisting that a creatively-biased child study sciences at University)

- **being compared unfavourably to others** – (e.g. *'Your sister would never have...'* or *'Other children in the world would be grateful for...'* or *'When we were your age, we never...'*)

- **being given the impression that their views or opinions are insignificant** – especially over matters which concern them (e.g. conversations about family holidays or their schooling that take place in their presence but without their involvement)

- **being deprived of a reasonable explanation** – especially when others are better informed (e.g. *'...because I say so'* or *'You wait till you're grown up, then you'll understand'*)

- **being given a label which devalues their individuality** (e.g. *'You girls are all the same'* or *'Kids – who'd have them?!'*)

- **being over-protected** – especially if they are given the impression that this is because they are particularly weak or stupid (e.g. *'No you can't go by yourself, because knowing you they'll take you for a ride'*)

- **over-punishing** – especially if they are given the impression that they are intrinsically bad (e.g. *'It's the only way to teach you a lesson – you're a born trouble-maker'*)

- **being given too few rules and guidelines** – especially if the lack of these causes the children to make numerous avoidable mistakes and then get put down for making them (e.g. not giving children adequate guidelines about sexual behaviour and then condemning them for making an embarrassing remark in public, or becoming pregnant; or not making a rule about playing with the matches and then getting cross when they burn themselves)

- **being on the receiving end of inconsistent behaviour** – especially if this is in their relationship with people who are responsible for their security (*e.g.* those children whose parents 'blow hot and cold' with their love and attention are often left with the feeling that there is something wrong with them which is preventing them from being consistently lovable or pleasing to be with)

- **being threatened with or receiving physical violence** – especially if they are told that they have driven the perpetrator to this immoral and undesirable act (e.g. *'You're the only person in the world who makes me feel violent'* or *'I feel awful about having hit you, but you're so difficult'*)

- **being subjected to inappropriate sexual innuendo or contact** – especially from someone entrusted to care for them (e.g. child sexual abuse from a relative, babysitter or teacher)

- **being blamed for leading a loved or respected person astray** (e.g. *'If you hadn't been so naughty in the supermarket I wouldn't have needed this cigarette'* or *'If I were teaching you I think I would have lost interest by now, too.'*)

- **being over-fed a diet of unachievable ideals by the media** – especially when they themselves are socially or physically disadvantaged and have very little hope of ever reaching perfection (e.g. seeing images on TV of other children who can afford to give up their toys or pocket money to the third world; or seeing pictures of clever ideas for Mother's Day gifts in magazines, when they may not have access to the materials needed to produce them, or even Mums who will appreciate them).

As I was writing this, memories from my own childhood came

flooding back – quite probably difficult emotional bells have started to ring for you, too. Maybe if you are a parent like me you may have identified not only with the children's experiences, but also with the imperfect guilty adults!

Perhaps we can take some comfort in reminding ourselves that we are not alone. In fact we are probably in the company of the vast majority because, even in today's psychologically enlightened world, these kinds of knocks to children's self esteem are still very commonplace. The good news is that there is hope for us yet, on both fronts! In the following chapters there are guidelines on how to heal your own childhood emotional wounds (Chapter 3) and guidelines on how to break unwanted habits which seem to compel us to knock rather than build others' self esteem (Chapter 9). But for the moment let's return to our discussion of how we acquire negative self esteem and other unwanted aspects of ourselves – because this knowledge can fuel our motivation to change.

What effect does the battering of a child's self esteem have on the formation of his or her personality? There are some people who still (in spite of much psychological evidence to the contrary) argue that this kind of emotional abuse can in fact have a *positive* effect (e.g. *'It helps toughen them up and prepare them for the real world'* and *'humility is after all an ennobling virtue'*).

Perhaps in *some* cultures, in *some* circumstances and with *some* children, one or two of the examples I have given could have a positive psychological effect. But the evidence strongly suggests that children whose self esteem has been *repeatedly* knocked in these ways are much more likely to enter adulthood with two very serious disadvantages:

1. **A *'victim'* style of personality** – deeply embedded in their psyche is the belief that life is destined to offer them only more discouragement and abuse – and furthermore that they are *powerless* to defend themselves from such injustice. In addition, because it is a psychological 'law' that like seeks like, they will find themselves unconsciously *drawn* towards experiences and relation-

ships which will confirm their view of themselves as losers, and of life as disappointing. Because they are not expecting 'the best' they may not even notice positive opportunities. If happiness does by chance enter their experience they always reserve a degree of suspicion and expect their 'unusual fortune' to be short-lived. Having such a negatively inclined view of their future, they tend to be very unmotivated to assert their needs or develop their potential for either success or happiness.

2. **A deficiency of social and life skills** – which means that they are *much less able* to behave automatically in ways which are self-protective, self-confident and self-empowering. For example, coming from the kind of childhood background we have identified is unlikely to have encouraged them to learn the important arts of speaking, acting and presenting themselves in ways that will ensure that they are noticed and respected. They may even find compliments and genuine appreciation embarrassing, simply because they do not know *how* to handle them assertively. Those who by nature are introverts are likely to be seen as painfully shy, those who are extroverts will be seen as too 'pushy' or 'loud'. Neither will find supportive nurturing relationships easy to form and maintain.

Such children, therefore, enter the adult world with noticeably *less personal power* than those who have had the growth of their self esteem encouraged and boosted. This means that in our current society they are also very much less able to achieve any other kind of power, including the basic economic power to earn a reasonable living.

Finally, these psychologically deprived and damaged children will find themselves very much less able to withstand even the normal wear and tear of adult emotional life.

How Self Esteem Can Be Dented and Battered in our Adult Lives

Unfortunately, even if we have had a charmed emotional childhood our self esteem still has a tough survival course to work through in modern everyday adult life. I am sure most of you can identify with many of these following examples as well!

Factors which can damage the self esteem of adults include:

- being taken for granted, ignored or rejected – especially by someone whom we like, love or respect
- being 'put-down' or unfairly criticized – especially in situations where it is difficult for us to defend ourselves (e.g. by a boss at work; a friend at a party; a barrister in court)
- shopping for clothes and finding nothing to fit us – especially when we seem to be surrounded by sales assistants and fellow shoppers of the 'Vogue' variety!
- coming out in 'unsightly' spots, rashes or sores – especially just before one of those daunting 'high profile' events!
- being 'herded' into an overcrowded train – especially when we have just bought our ticket from someone who gave us the impression that we look more like someone who could only afford to go by coach!
- an unexpected visit from certain relatives or friends when our house is a mess or the children are having an embarrassing tantrum
- being deceived – especially by someone in whom we had placed our trust
- failing an exam – especially one which everyone else in our world seems well able to pass!
- being turned down for a job or course – especially one which was well within our capabilities
- being left behind on our career ladder – especially when younger or less experienced people are skipping a few rungs

- doing boring, repetitive work – especially when it's of the kind we know could equally well be done by a mindless robot
- not receiving appreciation or just economic reward for our labours – especially when we seem to be surrounded by prosperous idlers
- not being consulted about changes to our working conditions or job description – especially when the 'reforms' do not appear to reflect our interests
- not being given fair opportunities to use our strengths and potential for taking responsibility
- being made redundant – especially at a time when we should have been working near the peak of our potential
- having our needs ignored or barely recognized when we are incapacitated or disabled
- making a mistake – especially one which we feel we should not have made
- doing something 'wrong' – especially if the deed breaches our own moral code

– and these are just some of the more common experiences which I know about! I am well aware that many of you will have experienced many more serious threats and damage, which may include, for example:

- prolonged unemployment or unjust redundancy
- persistent political or social discrimination
- sexual abuse
- violent attack to ourselves or our property
- serious deterioration of, or damage to, either body or mind.

And let's not forget the vicious cycle that can start as soon as we receive just any one (not to mention two or more!) of these knocks.

Although all the above experiences have the potential to hurt our self esteem, the extent of the damage caused by each individual knock will, of course, depend on a number of

17

variable factors, such as:

- the sheer *quantity* of blows – don't we all know the 'last straw' feeling?
- the current state of our basic, inner *sense of self-worth* which is, of course, substantially shaped and formed by the experiences our self esteem has met both in childhood and as adults
- our *physical health* – don't we all know how much more a put-down hurts when we are tired or 'off colour'?
- the quality of our *self-protective skills* which enable us to 'fight back' and assert ourselves
- the amount of *power and status* we currently have in each situation. For example, an unfair criticism from a peer is unlikely to have the same wounding power as that of a senior colleague who uses his or her power to humiliate us in the course of an important public meeting.

And finally, our ability to withstand each of these knocks will depend on just *how many* of these factors are currently in play. The low self esteem cycle is so vicious that it is not uncommon to find all five present at once!

It is therefore vital that those of us who find ourselves prone to getting caught up in such negative whirlpools know how to use efficient, purposeful and even sometimes *aggressive* strategies in defence of our self esteem.

It is going to be fun to watch and see how long the meek can keep the earth after they inherit it

KIN HUBBARD

With the odds for success and happiness so very heavily weighted against people with shaky self esteem, who can afford simply to sit back and patiently hope that Lady Luck or a guiding star will eventually bring a fair share of good fortune? So let's move into action!

Section 2
Laying the Foundations for Action

In this section we will be covering the background personal development work which I find most people need to do *before* they can make effective use of a self esteem building programme. Even if you have already done a considerable amount of work on yourself, I would suggest that you read quickly through this section as I shall be referring to many of the concepts and strategies discussed here in the practical exercises in Sections Three and Four.

2

Ten Golden Keys to Self Esteem

As I know that I always have more commitment to an activity if I can understand the purpose and philosophy behind what I am trying to do, in this chapter I will outline the basic principles behind this self esteem building programme. I have used a mnemonic based on the letters in the words SELF ESTEEM to make this bit of the theory easier to remember.

Scrutiny
Explanation
Love
Focus
Envisaging
Strategy
Triggers
Encouragement
Experimentation
Monitoring

Scrutiny

Before we begin making any change it is always advisable to make a detailed study of the current status quo. In the area of self esteem building work, this means taking steps to increase our own self-awareness and doing a thorough review of our lifestyle and relationships.

You may find that this is the most scary stage of all. People often think that once they start serious self-reflection they may get even more down and depressed. This only happens if there is no effective personal development programme to support the 'navel-gazing' work. You need not worry – I assure you this book contains enough ideas to help line the walls of your whole house with practical action plans!

Explanation

Once we have gathered our information we need to analyse it as objectively as we can. Taking a *logical* look at the facts helps us to clarify, accept and take responsibility for what we *can* change. That which we cannot change we are then more easily able to accept or delegate as the responsibility of others.

This aspect of our work often entails looking back into the past to gain some understanding of the present. Critical 'outsiders' often think that when we do this our main objective is to apportion blame. But certainly no one is on trial in this work. Any analysis we do is merely a small (albeit important) step in the process of helping us to increase *our* ability to take more responsibility (not less) for our own feelings and our future.

Love

This is the essential food of the whole programme! Self-love must be administered immediately and abundantly in very practical and clearly demonstrable ways. Ideally I would recommend a week locked in a luxurious health hotel before even reading the next chapter of this book! Most people could do with a boost to their physical energy before embarking on personal development work, but those of us with low self esteem are likely to have an even greater need of some extra physical care and nurturing.

But it isn't just at the start of the your programme that you will need to 'spoil yourself' with evidence of your self-love; your progress will benefit greatly if you keep taking substantial doses of this medicine throughout your work.

If you have grown up in the belief that this kind of love is sinful and immoral, you may need first to work on challenging the ethics and rationality behind this. If you are in the habit of confusing the ethics of self-love with selfishness, the exercises in Chapter 6 should help – but even once 'converted' you may still find yourself addicted to people-pleasing habits. You need to treat this infliction just as you would any other self-destructive habit (see Chapter 4).

Focus

Low self esteem causes so many problems in so many areas of our lives and relationships that it is easy to get overwhelmed or flit our attention anxiously from one area to another. It is, therefore, very important to focus on *one* manageable problem at a time; in so doing we not only greatly enhance our chance of success but also give ourselves the opportunity to enjoy and fully benefit from the confidence boost that accompanies each achievement.

Throughout your programme, therefore, you should focus on *one* problem at a time. The initial ones must be only mildly, rather than extremely challenging. (For example, you could choose to work on boosting your self esteem when you are in the company of certain people whom you do not *need* particularly to impress but with whom you would *like* to feel more comfortable and at ease. This means that you have a better chance of keeping your anxiety levels within manageable limits.)

I find that most people are desperate to dive in at the deep end of their problems. Resist this temptation by reminding yourself that the world of low self esteem is a dangerous whirlpool and not at all a friendly sea!

Envisaging

We can greatly increase our motivation if we constantly keep a clear image in the forefront of our minds of the new self-assured persona we are trying to acquire. You will find that in several programmes I suggest doing exercises which will help you to feed your subconscious with positive images of the 'you' you are trying to become. I have found that it also helps enormously if we share this dream image with other people. (Why not start now by telling at least one supportive friend that you are currently reading and working through this book, and letting him or her know what positive changes you envisage for yourself?)

Strategy

As I said earlier, strategies and even aggressive action plans are essential – but they must be broken down into *small, practical steps*. Often I will suggest a specific format for your action plan depending on the kind of work you are doing. But a golden rule for any of your programmes is always to be aware of at least *three specific and immediate goals*, as well as your long-term wider aims. Like the latter, these should be freely spoken about and always written down and placed where they can be readily and regularly viewed.

To give your strategy the very best chance of success, you will also need to back up your plans with excellent organization. The first step must be to show yourself that you 'mean business' by making your self esteem plans look like professional documents. Type them up if you can, or at the very least write them out in clear legible handwriting using highlighted headings and lists with bullet points or numbers. You should then date them and file them away (unless they can be pinned up for all to see!). I always suggest allocating, at the very least, a special folder or file for personal development work. (Why not stop reading and find one right now – even if it is only a temporary one?) You will then need to mark it *Private and Confidential* and place it in a safe place – but not one which is so well hidden that you yourself might forget it is there! Use this file to keep your written work in, and as a safe-haven for any other bits and pieces you may want to accumulate while working (e.g. ideas or observations jotted down on bits of paper at work, interesting photos, cartoons, articles, quotations, etc.)

Triggers

Breaking any habit is hard, but because low self esteem patterns often have been ingrained in childhood they can be tougher than most to overcome. Because these patterns are often conditioned responses they can sometimes be stimulated by simple associations with 'everyday' experiences. I'm sure most people know the feeling of 'shrivelling' one size smaller just on hearing a certain word, smelling the whiff of a particular aroma or even experiencing certain weather such as a storm. Even if we cannot completely 'brainwash' such responses into oblivion, identifying and naming them does demystify them, keeps us on our guard and prepares us for taking corrective action. (See particularly the strategy called 'Breaking Self-Destructive Habits' in Chapter 4.)

Encouragement

Because the process of personal development usually takes place at a 'plodding' rather than a 'breakneck' pace, it is more likely to be sustained if it is regularly bolstered by support. But in self esteem building work such support should, first and foremost, come from ourselves in the form of regular motivational treats. As most people with low self esteem tend to be mean in the way that they reward themselves, we usually need strong, efficient reminders. (A constructive job for a nagging friend?!)

Experimentation

As with every human learning process, the more individually tailored your development programme, the more likely it is to be successful. For example, throughout this book I suggest numerous exercises and give you many 'Do' and 'Don't' lists, but none of these should ever be treated as 'gospel truths'. I hope that you will be able to use my suggestions as starting points for your own experiments with a whole variety of behaviours and strategies. Although I have worked with people of all ages from a wide range of cultural backgrounds, I am still aware that some of the learning I have had from my experience will not be relevant to everyone reading this book. A suggestion which may prove to be invaluable 'advice' to one person may not be even remotely relevant for someone else. Unfortunately the only sure way of testing the usefulness of some of the strategies and guidelines will be through experimentation! Once you have tried them you can then adapt them to suit *your* particular personality, culture, circumstances, family, organization or relationships.

I know only too well that working in this way may prove to be more difficult than it sounds. When my self esteem was at a very low ebb, I can remember being insatiably greedy for infallible advice and strict guidelines. In fact, the shakier my self-confidence was, the more desperately I sought magic solutions from esteemed idols. But, of course, the very essence of self esteem building is about learning to have more respect for your own potential, skills and knowledge. One way to begin is to read and work through this book, always aware that *you are your own best guide and mentor* when it comes to shaping and selecting the behaviour, values and lifestyle which can build and boost your own self esteem.

Monitoring

Regular appraisal in any learning programme is essential and, as I have already implied, in this particular field the only judge and jury worth listening to is *you*. You will always need to build into your action plans time to do regular and thorough assessments of your progress. This is often difficult for people who have been suffering from low self esteem for a while because they may have lost their ability to make even the simplest self-appraisals. This is particularly true in the area of feelings. When our self esteem begins to dip, we tend (unconsciously) to adopt defensive psychological behaviours which ensure that we have neither the time, the energy nor the inclination to assess whether or not we like or love ourselves. Some of the most common defences which you may immediately recognize are:

- throwing ourselves into non-stop activity
- allowing ourselves to become exclusively passionate and exhaustingly caring for others or a 'good cause'
- focusing all our emotional energy on a particular fear, phobia or obsession
- deadening our senses with drink or drugs.

If any of this kind of activity is familiar to you, you may need to do some serious healing work before you can begin honestly and effectively to monitor your progress. The next chapter could therefore be a crucial one for you. After all, monitoring our self esteem should never be a wholly cerebral activity, it must be done by both our hearts and our heads – which can be exceedingly difficult if we are still emotionally crippled with a backlog of buried hurt and pain.

3

Strategy for Emotional Healing

A clay pot sitting in the sun will always be a clay pot. It has to go through the white heat of the furnace to become porcelain.

MILDRED WITTE STOUVEN

Emotional pain is the basic food of low self esteem junkies. It often seems that the more they get the more they crave. Like any other addicts, the victims eventually cry out for more and more, kidding themselves that they have risen above its power to hurt ('Go on, spit in my face, I don't care anymore').

The reality is that emotionally broken hearts hurt just as much as the physically damaged ones and they can be just as disabling and life-threatening. So why in our culture is there such a distinct difference in the way they are commonly treated? Rarely do psychological wounds receive a comparable amount of healing attention.

The answer, I believe, is not always that people care any less about emotionally hurt hearts, it is simply that in our culture they are very often *much less informed* about what they can *usefully* do to help heal the wound. Once the 'tea and sympathy' approach has been tried and found wanting, the only other options most sufferers believe to be available are patience, distraction, or costly psychotherapy.

Perhaps any one or a mixture of all these options may satisfactorily 'cure' minor emotional bumps and scratches, but they are usually grossly inadequate remedies for the degree of psychological pain which tends to inhabit the hearts of people with low self esteem. They tend to have had their feelings hurt so often, and so deeply, that they could literally spend a lifetime awaiting the uncertain healing mercies of Father Time. (And in the mean time their self esteem weakens and weakens and the vicious addictive cycle revolves again and again.)

As a direct result of my own difficulty in healing a deep emotional wound of my own, a few years ago I began to take a special interest in this subject. I spent a considerable amount of time observing and noting the specific processes which seem to promote efficient emotional recovery. Eventually I began to gain a much clearer idea of what I believe we can ourselves do to encourage more efficient healing of psychological pain.

Most significantly, I discovered that there seems to be a series of *seven predictable stages* we can help ourselves work through step by step. The first five seem to be particularly *essential* to the emotional healing process; the final two are more like *welcome bonuses* because they give us a boost of *additional*, but not necessarily crucial psychological strength. In a 'normal', healthy healing process it seems that these stages may sometimes overlap, but I have never yet felt or observed anything being gained from trying to work through them in a different order.

To make this developing 'theory' easier to discuss and translate into a practical strategy I eventually decided to call each of these identifiable stages by the following names:

1. Exploration
2. Expression
3. Comfort
4. Compensation
5. Perspective

6. Channelling
7. Forgiveness

During the last couple of years I have talked about these stages to hundreds of people with whom I have worked, and I have been told very many times that just hearing the mere outline of the process has had some immediate healing impact. I suppose this should not surprise me because I have always found that once I can clearly see the road I need to take to work through any problem, I know I am well on the way to recovery. So I trust that simply by gaining some understanding of the theory you too will get an immediate boost of motivational hope and will feel more inclined to test out the strategy.

I have also found that this theory can be a very useful *diagnostic* tool because it helps us to pinpoint the exact stage we have reached in our healing process. This makes it easier for us to plan the next step more effectively. Discussing it can reveal the point where someone may have become emotionally 'stuck', because it often becomes very obvious that he or she may have skipped one of the essential stages.

In the not-too-distant future I will be expanding these thoughts into a book in their own right, but in view of the importance of emotional healing to the maintenance of high self esteem I am offering you an introduction to the strategy in the belief that it will be a useful, if not fully satisfying, *hors d'oeuvre*!

Why Is Emotional Healing So Difficult?

People with low self esteem experience great difficulty with emotional healing for two main reasons. First, they are likely to suffer generally from *an above-average amount of disappointment and loss*. As we have already noted, their negative attitudes and self-destructive behaviour ensure that they repeatedly fail to achieve success and happiness even when all the other odds are stacked in their favour.

Secondly, it is likely that they will find themselves on the receiving end of *an above-average amount of physical and emotional abuse* simply because they are such 'easy targets' for aggressors and manipulators. And, being notoriously inept at distinguishing the sheep from the wolves, we know that they often (however unwittingly) present themselves as victims over and over again.

Not only do people with low self esteem tend to meet a greater *number* of hurts, they usually also feel *more intense pain* when they are wounded. One reason is that their subconscious is often harbouring *an above-average store of unhealed wounds*. These old emotional hurts are readily reactivated whenever the 'salt' of a new hurt happens to be applied to one of their many festering Achilles' heels. For example, a critical appraisal at work will undoubtedly hurt much more if it happens to tap into the misery of unfulfilled potential, and a letter of rejection will disappoint more deeply if it meets a heart which is beginning to crack under the strain of a lifetime of 'brush-offs'.

But the agony rarely ends even there. On finding themselves experiencing pain which is so obviously disproportionate to their current hurt, people with low self esteem will then frequently turn the knife in on themselves. Instead of giving some healing expression to their tortured feelings, they often hastily swallow them and begin to batter themselves with self-reproach (e.g. *'I hate myself for being such a "cry-baby"'* or, *'It's my own fault for being so stupidly touchy'*).

Perhaps it's obvious how such a cycle of self-destructive behaviour can then itself have a disastrous knock-on effect to self esteem. But if you need any more convincing, read this depressingly familiar (only slightly exaggerated!) example.

John (who has a childhood history of being taunted by a bullying teacher for his 'over-enthusiastic' approach) is attending an important company meeting at which the Directors plan to allocate a new project. Because of his particular professional expertise and knowledge, John has every chance of being given this exciting opportunity. During the course of the meeting, a senior colleague makes a jovial, whispered tease about the size of John's presentation folder. On hearing the remark, John –

→feels a surge of rage
→becomes aware that his depth of feeling seems strangely inappropriate
→inwardly blames his own over-sensitivity
→bites his tongue and smiles
→inwardly flagellates his own self esteem with punitive and de-powering self-talk (e.g. *'What an over-sensitive wimp, why do you always rise to the bait?'*)
→as a result, his anxiety mounts and he loses his concentration
→he misses the one 'golden opportunity' to put forward his well-researched presentation
→a junior colleague gets allocated this important new work
→on leaving the meeting, the senior colleague makes a jibe about his unopened bulging folder
→John leaves the meeting feeling a total failure as well as a wimp
→he is so ashamed and perplexed by his own behaviour that he buries his deep disappointment and burning resentment, and brushes off the comforting (and potentially healing) commiserations of his friends with a façade of jokey nonchalance.

Not only did this sequence of events hurt the career development and self esteem of a talented and hard-working individual, but it was counter-productive for the interests of his company – and possibly the national economy of his country as well! So perhaps this next section should be compulsory reading for all treasury officials and managing directors!

How We Can Heal Old Emotional Wounds

...we could never learn to be brave and patient if there were only joy in the world.

HELEN KELLER

Essentially our strategy is a series of constructive action plans designed to guide us through the emotional healing process which should, ideally, have taken place soon after each wound was incurred.

Let's start with reminding ourselves of the five essential and two bonus stages. I have devised a mnemonic sentence to help fix the names and their order in your mind (see page 34). (The sentence could be pinned up somewhere as an encouraging reminder of your positive goal.)

Ideally, each stage should be worked though step by step, but in your real world it is likely that there will often need to be some overlap. However an important point to remind yourself of from time to time is that *the healing process will not work efficiently if you try to go too quickly or if you skip a stage or two*. I have found that a favourite trick of people with low self esteem is to try to rush headlong to No 7 – i.e. FORGIVE-NESS. This is a habit which they have probably had since early childhood. Maybe at that time the 'goodies' required for other stages were not available, or perhaps they *needed* the safety and approval that FORGIVENESS can undoubtedly bring in the short term. If you find yourself tempted to skip or rush, remind yourself that this habit cannot begin to compete with the *long-term* boost to your self esteem which genuine Emotional Healing can bring.

Before reading through the following guide to the strategy, take a little time to reflect on some of the minor and major emotional hurts you have received in the course of your life. If you can select one or two of your own unhealed emotional wounds to use as examples, the following guidelines will

make much more sense for you. But remember, when choosing, that these wounds come in all shapes and sizes and that what will feel like a wound to one person at a certain time in life will be 'water off a duck's back' to another at any time. (If your memory needs a little jogging you could reread the list of examples of knocks to self esteem in our childhood – pages 11-13 – and our adulthood – pages 16-17.)

It is often a good idea to choose one relatively minor hurt and another which is likely to require more sophisticated action. To illustrate the strategy I have chosen two very different examples from my own childhood – but don't forget that yours could be taken also from much more recent adult experiences.

Example A
Disappointment arising from not being selected for the school tennis team

Example B

Hurt from being inadequately loved by a parent

At the end of each section I will offer some appropriate action for each example, and I suggest that you do the same for the wounds which you have selected.

Stage 1: Exploration

There is no coming to consciousness without pain.

CARL JUNG

Our first task is to explore the nature of our hurt and *openly acknowledge* what we *perceive* to have happened. The natural way children seem to do this is by first *thinking through* what happened and then *telling someone* about the experience. e.g. 'Mum   I didn't get selected for the team today, but Jane did.' Other ways children spontaneously explore their hurts include play-acting what happened, or painting a picture or creating a story about it.

By the time we reach adulthood, very often our immediate reaction may be to repress these natural healing responses and put what happened to the back of our minds. In fact, there could sometimes be a very good reason for doing so (e.g. we are too busy writing a letter of complaint or trying to find another job), but often our 'good reason' is far from positive (e.g. a determination to smile sweetly through all manner of adversity, or a belief that no one has time to listen to us).

Unfortunately, once a hurt has been relegated to the back shelves of our minds, that's very often where it stays. Even those of us with immense 'psychological know-how' are often tempted to leave troublesome memories well alone, especially when the practical issues relating to the problem have already been solved.

As I am writing this chapter there is a heated battle being

raged in both the courts and the media about the validity of memories relating to childhood abuse which emerge during therapy. The concern is that *some* therapists may be digging their unscrupulous way into the subconscious world of suggestible clients and planting false recollections. Theoretically this is of course possible, but I do not think it should worry the very vast majority of us who want to explore and heal from our emotional past. After all, the *objective* with this stage of the strategy is *not* to allocate blame and plan retribution, but merely *to explore our subjective memories so that we have a clear idea of what emotional damage has been done and can begin to take restorative action.* So, in fact, it may be just as important to talk about our *perceptions* of what happened when we were hurt, and about our *imagined explanations*, because they may have been just as emotionally damaging as any 'real truth'. The paralysing fear that we feel if we *think* we are going to be hit is not very different from the fear we feel before we actually *are* hit – *both* have the capacity to cause emotional wounds.)

If you experience difficulty in recollecting painful memories (especially concerning someone you may love or have loved), it often helps to make *a clear distinction between the people in our memories and their behaviour.* For example, it was not 'Dad' (the whole person) who may have emotionally damaged me, but just an aspect of his *parenting behaviour*. I am aware that, to a casual observer of exploratory work in therapy sessions, we do sometimes appear to be 'blaming' a particular person or group of people, especially when participants are encouraged to 'speak their mind' to chairs, cushions or people representing the 'offenders'. But these are merely techniques to enable people with deeply buried hurt to break through into the first few stages of the emotional healing process.

Sometimes it helps to remind ourselves that:

– first, we are exploring *perceptions and fantasies rather than the real truth of what may actually have occurred.*
– secondly, emotional healing very often *improves* the relationship between the people concerned because it encourages the growth of genuine forgiveness.

Possible Action

Example A
Recount the story to an understanding tennis-loving friend

Example B
Look through a childhood photo album with my sister to rekindle old memories

> *The goal of recounting the trauma story is integration, not exorcism.*
>
> Judith Lewis Herman

Stage 2: Expression

We are healed from suffering only by experiencing it to the full.
MARCEL PROUST

Once we have given ourselves the opportunity to explore our memories, we should find ourselves moving on quite naturally to the next stage. This one is about allowing ourselves to *feel the feelings* connected to the hurt and find some safe way to give them expression.

We can, of course, easily observe the healing powers of free emotional expression in very young children. They will quite naturally cry when they are sad, scream when they are hurt, and bang about when they are jealous. Five minutes later, typically, they will be happily playing once again with the perpetrator. But as we grow older we have to learn to curb our spontaneity and control the flow of these feelings. Ideally, we will be taught (usually indirectly through role-models) how to find ways of temporarily containing them and then, later, healthily releasing them in appropriate places and at appropriate times.

Unfortunately, however, most of us do not receive such excellent tuition in emotional management. Instead we find much less satisfactory ways of coping with our difficult feelings. Commonly in our culture we learn to *disengage* from them, as we observe adults 'biting their tongues', 'swallowing their pride' and 'choking back' their tears. These habits then become firmly embedded into our 'normal' behaviour patterns and are further reinforced as we are praised for being 'nice', 'quiet', 'well-mannered' and 'brave'. (This is, of course, especially true for those of us with low self esteem whose experiences in childhood have left us with an above-average 'need to please'.)

Understandably, therefore, this second healing stage can be quite frightening and daunting. Many people find that they are reluctant to encourage contact with emotions which they have always felt were 'too hot to handle'. If you find yourself having a similar reaction, remind yourself that the main objective of EXPRESSION is to experience only a limited *degree of re-engagement* with the feeling. The grand histrionic catharsis that the old Hollywood movies so often imply are essential to psychological healing are not required by this strategy! In fact, I often find that it is quite sufficient for most people to feel just a mere 'trickle of tears' or a small 'pang of jealousy'. But of course, there are a small minority of others who have such a backlog of deep unhealed wounds that will feel the need to express more of the repressed hurt before they can complete this stage. Usually (but not always) I would advise these people to seek the help of a therapist or counsellor who will provide them with safe space for cathartic release, and who can be there for them when they are ready to move on to the next stage.

Possible Action

Example A
While taking a long hot bath, replay the scenes of school tennis and allow the tears to flow if they come

Example B
Read a moving autobiography of someone who has had a similar experience, or play some emotive music while looking through the photo album again. Allow the sadness or anger to surface slowly

Stage 3: Comfort

> *Recovery can take place only in the context of relationships; it cannot occur in isolation...sharing the traumatic experience with others is a precondition for the restitution of a sense of a meaningful world.*
>
> JUDITH LEWIS HERMAN

This stage involves experiencing the soothing powers of being 'held' either physically, or metaphorically, by a *genuinely caring, non-judgemental person who empathizes with our hurt.* Sometimes it may be enough for the comforter merely to provide a peaceful 'reassuring presence' while we gently, and naturally, recover our own emotional equilibrium. But often it may also be appropriate for them to indicate their care and concern in a more physical way (by, for example, providing a cup of tea or even a cuddle!).

If your wound has involved being *unjustly* hurt or even abused and your comforter reacts to your 'story' with sympathetic and appropriate shock and horror, his or her contribution could be 'super-healing'. This is especially true if your hurt took place in childhood. Because children are naturally egocentric, when they are emotionally hurt they automatically think that the fault must be theirs. So unless they are told *in no uncertain terms that the blame should lie elsewhere, they will assume it is their responsibility.* Indeed, this is how the self esteem of most people with whom I work first began to crumble.

For many of us, who have a long history of low self esteem, much of our emotional wounding was originally caused (wittingly or unwittingly) by parent-figures. Very frequently our parents may not only have refused to acknowledge responsibility for the hurts they gave us directly, but they may actually have blamed *us* for being the kind of child who attracted or deserved that kind of hurt from other people as well. How much more emotionally strong we could have been if only we had had even our simple everyday hurts healed by the kind of parent I describe in this following example! (Note I have accentuated the natural examples of COMFORT in action.)

A toddler is happily playing in a public park with some friends, when suddenly a man taking a short-cut across the playing field to the station rushes past the group of children and, in so doing, knocks the young toddler flying onto the ground. The child is not physically hurt but is shocked and frightened. He runs to his mother who is standing nearby; he tells her what has happened. He says he's frightened that the man will come again *and he wants to go home. His mother says she **knows how he feels** and gives him a **comforting cuddle**. He **cries** in her arms for a few minutes while **listening to reassurances that it was not his fault** (e.g. 'That silly man should not having been rushing and he should have been keeping to the path – I'll stand and watch and make sure that he, or anyone else, can't do it again.') A few minutes later the child has completely recovered his confidence and has returned to play.*

I hope you have perhaps witnessed similar scenes, because this will give you at least you some idea of what working through this stage involves.

I have often found, however, that at this stage people with low self esteem let out a cry of hopeless despair. They cannot believe that there are willing and able comforters anywhere within *their* reach. The truth is that there is usually a choice of hundreds! *Most human beings (even if they do not obviously 'look the type') will willingly offer this kind of assistance. But, very often, in this frenetic modern world even the kindest and most sensitive people may need to be asked.* Furthermore, to ensure a positive response to our request for COMFORT we must ask in an assertive, direct way which clearly spells out the limits of the help we require. Many people (simply out of fear) will run a mile if they think that you may need a major emotional rescue, but that's certainly not what this stage in this self-help strategy requires.

Possible Action

Example A
A 'good old moan' over a couple of pints with a friend

Example B
An abundance of empathic sharing and hugs from like-minded friends who have had similar experiences. (An esteem building self help group?)

Stage 4: Compensation

Now we are reaching the more satisfying and rewarding stages. I am sure that you will welcome the news that this is the time when we can quite *justifiably* and *purposefully* submerge ourselves in treats and hedonistic pleasure! But before you rush off to book yourself that luxury cruise in the Bahamas, remember that in order to give yourself high-quality, lasting COMPENSATION, most people will need more than a temporary dose of self-indulgence.

The objective of this stage is to try to find a way of *'making up to yourself'* for the hurt you have received.

Once again let's turn to a practical example of a good parent demonstrating this stage and its healing work. It's a scenario that anyone who has looked after children in a British-style summer knows only too well. Once again I have highlighted the healing aspects.

A child is promised a day out in the park and then the day arrives and it rains, and rains! For five minutes or so Mum allows the child to cry or shout abuse (at the clouds!); then offers a comforting cuddle or drink – and when the tears are almost spent, suggests a compensatory experience (e.g. playing a game or inviting a friend to tea). Although the game or tea-party does not have the thrill of the park, nonetheless it does manage to take the sting out of the disappointment and help it eventually to dissipate.

Now let's look at the alternative scenario which has, I'm afraid, much more the kind of tone that people with low self esteem can recognize.

It rains – the child cries, whines or stamps his foot. His Mum, (her temples tightening at the thought of being cooped up with 'screaming kids' all day), gives him a quick 'clip' and says 'You're giving me a headache – don't make a fuss – it's only a picnic you're missing. One day you'll learn, life's always like that. If you make a plan, something's bound to spoil it. There's no point in crying – it's me who should be crying – I've just got so much to do, I'll be so glad when the school holidays are through. Go and tidy your room, it's in a terrible mess – that'll take you the best part of the morning anyway. If you stay in here, you'll just get on my nerves.'

It is very likely that the boy in the latter story will grow up without having a clue what this COMPENSATION business is all about! As an adult, his first task at this stage would thus be some *experimenting with the 'good life'!* As with many people with low self esteem, it might take him some months to find out what kind of 'treats' would work as recompense for *him*.

(Even emotional healing can be fun!)
When you begin your programme of COMPENSATION, remember that it must not only fit the person, but also the

degree and nature of the hurt. For example, the hurt from under-achievement at school may need a University course as compensation, or the pain from losing a mother too early may require a lifetime of extra-nurturing friendships.

Possible Action

Example A
Treat myself to a course of superior tennis coaching

Example B
Spend more time with nurturing friends and plan how to become a more loving 'parent' to myself (better food, a ban on self-put-downs, etc.)

> *The deepest personal defeat suffered by human beings is constituted by the difference between what one was capable of becoming and what one has in fact become.*
>
> ASHLEY MONTAGU

Stage 5: Perspective

> *Life is a series of experiences, each one makes us bigger, even though sometimes it is hard to realize this.*
>
> HENRY FORD

This is the stage which every intellectual loves, because this is the time when it *is* helpful to *think*, in order to make some sense of what has happened. Our hearts are well on their way to being mended and we are probably getting restless to move on into the future. But it is much easier to put the hurt of the past firmly behind us if we first assess what *positive* aspects we can 'salvage' from our old wound to take forward with us.

But don't worry, I am not suggesting that each of your hurts merits a thesis or a working party report (though of course some of the more serious ones may!). Usually a fairly brief objective review will suffice, because our goal remains very *personal*. Its main purpose is *to be able to see the hurt in its various surrounding contexts so that we can, at the very least, say to ourselves 'I have learned something useful'.*

I have found that we can often 'kick-start' ourselves into this stage by reflecting on these kinds of questions:

- Were the particular circumstances of my wound extraordinary or commonplace? Am I likely to meet these again? – If so, when and where?
- Was the behaviour of the person or people involved unusual or typical?
- Is there anything which *I* did which may have been a contributory factor? – If so, do I want to make sure I do not do it again, or am I unable, or unwilling (because perhaps I do not consider it is wrong) to change my behaviour?
- Is this a hurt which others have experienced? – If so, are there contributory factors in society which may also share some of the responsibility? Would it help to talk to other people about their experiences? (It usually does!) Would it help to read a book or see a film on the subject?
- What personal strengths did I draw on which helped me to survive through this hurt at the time it occurred?
- Were there any aspects of my behaviour which were not so helpful?
- Where does this experience stand in relation to my whole life history and plans for the future? Is it highly significant or very minor? Have I been regarding it as though it was more, or less, significant than it is?
- What is the main lesson I have learned about myself?
- What have I learned about other people?
- What have I learned about life in general?!
- Is there anything else I need or want to do before I move

on? Do I want to re-negotiate a relationship? Do I need to do more work on any of the earlier stages in this healing process?

Finally, I want to emphasize that as we are working through PERSPECTIVE, it is important not to lose sight of the overall objective of this whole emotional healing strategy. Its purpose is to heal *your* personal hurt. As you are working through this stage, in particular, it's so easy for people with low esteem to get side-tracked into putting the needs of others (including the 'baddies' who were involved) way above their own. Once you have regained your emotional strength and you are able to maintain your self esteem at a consistently high level, there will be plenty of time to turn your caring attention elsewhere! (See Chapter 9, for instance.)

Possible Action

Example A
Make a list of my sporting achievements since that time!

Example B
Do an evening class in the psychology of child development or make a list of the personal qualities which have enhanced my personality as a result of the experience (e.g. increased sensitivity to others' pain; ability to be independent, etc.)

What doesn't kill me makes me stronger.

ALBERT CAMUS

Stage 6: Channelling

Adversity reveals genius.

HORACE

You will not have to look very hard to find an example of this CHANNELLING stage doing its good work – you are currently reading one! I have now no doubt that in writing this book I am taking yet another step forward in the healing of my own very deeply-rooted emotional wounds. The particular nature of my work has given me a very convenient outlet for channelling the learning acquired from my own hurts into constructive use. Each time I find that I am able to use the wisdom gained from my own pain to help others deal with theirs, I am *thrice* rewarded. First, I get the natural human pleasure of seeing someone heal; secondly I get a sense of personal satisfaction from 'doing a good job well'; and thirdly I get a boost of psychological strength from having my own hurt healed even more. Is it any wonder that I constantly struggle with workaholism!?

But I have not included this stage in an attempt to encourage everyone who has been emotionally hurt to rush out and become a therapist or writer. Certainly, many people with my kind of background can (either as a volunteer or as a professional) do well in my field – but many do not and never will. In fact, I would think that the vast majority of people are not temperamentally suited to such work, and are likely to have much more aptitude for other just as important activities.

The objective of CHANNELLING is about finding *constructive ways of using any of the positive benefits we gain as a result of our hurtful experience and its subsequent healing process.* These could, for example, be one or all of the following:

– some specific knowledge or wisdom
– a boost of physical energy (we naturally get this on emotional recovery)
– increased psychological strength (we inevitably gain

from the combination of survival plus emotional health)
- increased sensitivity and awareness of others' emotional pain
- financial or other material gain we accrue as a result of any of the above
- increased power and influence as a result of our experiences.

The outlets which people find useful for CHANNELLING are as various as the kinds of people who get emotionally hurt. These outlets may be found in their work, social or family life, or through their religion or political party. Some people may find that through their personal experiences they can help thousands or millions (e.g. by starting campaigns or self-help organizations). Others may find that they want to concentrate their energies into helping just one or two people (perhaps their own children or elderly parents). Others may have much less obviously helpful outlets, but nevertheless their renewed energy, awareness and personal strength are being used to make them a better salesperson, teacher, team player, secretary, travel agent, artist, managing director – or simply a more caring world citizen.

It is important to remember that CHANNELLING is very different from throwing yourself into activity to 'dull' the pain of emotional hurt soon after it occurs. Although I can see the need for some people to do this sometimes, this kind of displacement activity is not to be recommended as a regular habit, because in the long term, as we have already noted, repressing emotional hurt is harmful to both ourselves and others. On the other hand, CHANNELLING the gains from emotional recovery can be a positive and creative experience with potential rewards for everyone! Furthermore, it is the final step in 'getting even' with the emotional wounds which have been stopping us from being the kind of person we want to be and living the kind of life we want and *deserve*.

I am writing this on the historic and moving day of Nelson Mandela's inauguration to the presidency of South Africa. Surely he must be one of the supreme examples of CHAN-

NELLING in action, and its power to enable us to move on into the next and final healing stage.

Possible Action

Example A
Do some voluntary coaching for young people at the local Sports Centre

Example B
Become a fund-raiser for a children's charity

> *It is far easier to forgive an enemy after you have got even with him.*
>
> OLIN MILLER

Stage 7: Forgiveness

Now we have landed in the realm of the saints – or have we?! I am not sure. But I do know that I have seen too many people suffering needlessly because they cannot find the 'divine' version of this wondrous substance, forgiveness, in their hearts. By this I mean the kind of forgiveness which requires us humbly to turn the other cheek while the wounded one is still bleeding and the abuser is still poised for attack. This is the kind that I hear preached about not only from the pulpits, but also, increasingly, on the lips and in the books of so many well-meaning therapists. It is now being sold not only as our ticket to an after-life of heaven, but also our guarantee of self-worth and inner peace in this wicked world!

I find this trend particularly alarming, not only because my own moral code deems some unrepented abuse and gross injustice still unforgivable, but also because it renders people with low self esteem and shaky mental health even more vulnerable. While in this state, they are often so desperate to please that they will ignore both their own moral code and their own emotional healing needs and rush headlong into forgiving those who have hurt them, and are likely to continue to hurt them. When they then realize they cannot *genuinely* forgive, they feel that *they* themselves are to blame and so their self esteem plummets even further!

So this stage is not about that kind of 'phony' forced forgiveness, it is more about the kind which arises very naturally and spontaneously when someone has worked through these stages and *wants* to say to the offender something like this:

> *I did not like what you did – it hurt me and (if you can assure me that you do not want it to happen again) I would like to shake hands, wipe the slate clean, and then I would like to re-negotiate our relationship so that it does not happen again.*

I am well aware that this FORGIVENESS stage is often hard to reach and work through, not because the 'victim' isn't ready or willing, but because the 'offender' does not want forgiveness or is unavailable (or dead). But fortunately this is a bonus and *not* an essential stage, and I do not believe that we need to feel either morally or emotionally disabled just because we cannot always reach its pearly gates!

Possible Action

Example A
No action may be required but some people might feel a sense of forgiveness towards either the team captain or even their inner 'young child' who may have hated him- or herself for not being a good enough 'sport'

Example B

Talk through this experience of healing with my parents, saying that I now want to put it behind me and start to rebuild a more mutually supportive and understanding relationship with them

Finally, don't forget –

Every Emotional Cut Can Produce Creative Fruit!

4

Strategy for Breaking Self-destructive Habits

To fall into a habit is to cease to be.

MIGUEL DE UNAMUNO

Do you often find that your behaviour is your own worst enemy? Do you hear yourself regularly saying:

'I wish I didn't always...'
'If only I could stop...'
'I can't help it, I always...'
'I couldn't stop myself...'

If you do, I suggest that a battle with your self-destructive habits must be a priority. After all, there is very little point in doing all the other self esteem building work in this book if, in the end, such behaviour has more control over you than *you* have!

The encouraging news is that if you have tried and failed many times to break free of these habits you should now find the task very much easier. Now, at least you and your unconscious should be pulling in the same direction – forward! With your self esteem improved you'll also find you have a lot more motivation, as well as more energy with which to fight your negative compulsions. When we enter any fray while our self esteem is at a low ebb, we often (without realizing it) set ourselves up for failure and give up too quickly.

The saints are the sinners who keep on going.
ROBERT LOUIS STEVENSON

I am very aware that ultimately habit-breaking seems me to be a highly *individualistic* art. Isn't it true that once we announce to the world that we want to break a certain habit we are suddenly inundated with 'unique' tips and 'pet theories'? In fact, it is easy to get overwhelmed and eventually cynical when your ears are ringing with Aunt Jane saying 'The only answer is to go cold turkey and give up NOW, for ever,' while Jon at the office swears by 'a rubber band on your wrist', your sister says 'a hypnotherapist is what you want,' your best friend sings the praises of her magazine's step-by-step plan, your chemist neighbour recommends the latest pill, the 'anon' group urges instant membership...and, now Gael Lindenfield starts pushing her latest strategy!

Needless to say I have no wish to preach to the converted among you, so if you already have your own set of magic habit-breaking tricks, please feel free to skip this chapter. *But*, before passing this chapter by, ensure that you have set your favourite formula to work. If on the other hand you are still looking for the trick to beat all tricks, why not try this new strategy which is (like so many of its rivals!) just a repackaged version of tried and tested 'old tricks'?

I have selected out my own favourite bits of the theory and some of the main tips which I use and frequently share with my clients, and parcelled them up in the guise of a 'battle strategy'. Although I am generally quite a pacifist by nature, when the survival of self esteem is threatened by self-sabotage, I do firmly believe that a war-like approach is both justified and imperative. I hope that the professional soldiers among you will be tolerant of the 'poetic licence' I have taken with your art and craft!

Strategy for the Battle of the Bad Habits

Survey the Enemy Field

Become your own spy. In your little (or large!) black book which you carry constantly with you, keep a note of all your individual sins against your self esteem. *Catalogue* with care all the occasions when you notice yourself thinking or acting against your own rules and values and working against your own interests. No doubt you will find your enemies, dressed in many different guises and loitering with intent in several areas of your life and relationships. Your inventory could, perhaps, include just a few of these common trespasses:

- skipping exercise routines
- smoking, eating or drinking too much
- eating too much junk food
- biting nails or scratching spots
- getting up (or going to bed) too late
- over-working
- becoming too tired to read your novel or do your hobby
- not bothering to make the effort to go out for pure fun
- not taking lunch breaks
- leaving things to the last minute
- keeping your home or desk/workspace in a mess
- compulsive unnecessary cleaning, tidying or double-checking
- saying 'sorry' too often
- not speaking up in meetings
- slipping into 'wall-flower mode' at parties or conferences
- talking too much or too quickly
- letting others start up or run conversations
- always putting forward the negative possibilities
- spending more than you earn
- not spending money you can afford to spend

– forgetting people's birthdays
– telling too many corny jokes.

Assess the Threat

Grade your list carefully *according to each item's threat to your self esteem* and sense of well-being, placing each habit in one of these categories:

1. lethal
2. highly dangerous
3. dangerous
4. mildly dangerous
5. potentially dangerous
6. a nuisance.

Select an Easy Target

Choose just *one* enemy habit to obliterate or imprison first. This will allow you time to warm up and polish your fighting skills *without too much risk* being involved.

> In releasing yourself from the bondage of bad habits, don't try
> to do all of them at once...Build on the strength of each
> victory. As the saying goes, 'It's a cinch by the inch, but it's
> hard by the yard.'
> JOHN ROGER AND PETER MCWILLIAMS

Search for Allies

Don't go in for lone pioneering unless you have to. Look for allies *with the same enemies* who are equally committed to the fight and whom you can trust to support and encourage you. This could mean, for example, pairing up with a friend who shares your bad habit, or joining a *successful* self-help group.

Appoint Your Strongest Generals

Assess which of your *personal strengths* could be of most use to you in leading this particular campaign. These could include, for example, your:

- *analytical brain*, which will plan a very detailed 'scientifically correct' strategy, the results of which can be easily anlaysed and monitored
- *humorous side*, which will be able to help keep the whole operation fun and not allow it to become too tedious and boring
- *nurturing qualities*, which could be entrusted with giving priority to your welfare and health
- *creativity*, which could be used for coming up with imaginative new tactics and tools
- *pragmatic side*, which could be used to keep your feet firmly on the ground and not get too carried away and provoke unnecessary challenges.

Select a Slogan

Choose one which will inspire you, especially in times of stress. If you are short of ideas, why not try this wonderful one which I heard recently

Vision without action is but a dream
Action without vision just passes the time
Vision with action can change the world.

or a very simple affirmation statement such as this one:

It may be hard but it's not impossible.

Map Out Your Overall Strategy

Commit your strategy to paper. Make it as colourful and interesting to look at as you can. But make sure that it is in keeping
with your campaign style and that it looks motivating and
well organized. Pin it up where you can see it and adjust it easily. Use *charts and graphs* if they have impact with you, but if
you are more creatively inclined you could draw an *impressive
picture* to illustrate your proposed campaign (perhaps an
adventure trail?).

Marshal Your Resources

Make a note of the assets you already have which will help
you fight this particular destructive habit, and work out how
you are going to acquire any more may need. *Set dates* immediately for begging, borrowing or buying these. For example:

1. Tuesday – ring Jean to borrow book on Time Management
2. Friday – apply for bank loan
3. Saturday – buy felt-tip pens to colour my strategy chart
4. Saturday – buy nicotine patches
5. Christmas – ask for radio alarm
6. Tonight – beg the family to do extra chores this month
7. Tomorrow – put in requisition for more new software.

Fly the Flag and Declare War

Tell the world that you are going to war, why you are going,
and the date you expect to win. (You don't have to divulge the
secrets of your strategy, especially to people who might enjoy
sabotaging it!) Design yourself a *logo* to symbolize your campaign – you then 'flag it up' in all sorts of places as a constant
reminder.

Take Up a Mascot

Defeating this kind of habit will most certainly bring welcome

change, but the battle through the transition stages may at times be quite scary because:

a) We may have to let go of the comfort and security of the enemy habit (even the worst ones have some kind of positive pay-off, which is often why they are so hard to conquer).

b) The new routine/relationship or behaviour may not bring *immediate* rewards.

A mascot can be used like a child's *'transitional object'* (the name which psychologists give to a comforting object that a child clings to in times of stress, such as the obligatory teddy, the scruffy piece of unwashed blanket, the special toy soldier or comic, etc.). I often suggest to clients that they secretly carry around a small object to remind them of their goal, and they have found that it gives them a feeling of comfort at times when their 'super-bravery' begins to quiver. (You may be interested to know that at the moment I am taking some of my own medicine! In my purse I am carrying around a small picture of Oprah Winfrey as my 'mascot', because I am currently waging war against a deeply entrenched habit that is sabotaging my chances of getting increased coverage in the media. Would you like to know more about my strategy and how the picture of Oprah helps? Well, if you would you will have to guess because I am reserving my right not to tell you – it's my secret!)

Plan the First Attack

You have chosen your easy target, so you ought to make your first attack very soon or your troops will lose heart! Make sure that there is a challenging task to accomplish within the *first week* (and no later) of your battle. Try to ensure that this is a manoeuvre which will bring instant inspiring victory. For example:

- one complete day without...
- one complete room re-organized
- three days in a row of being on time.

Assess Enemy Tactics

A clue to these may lie in the list you made in your black book when your were in your role as in-house spy. In this battle your worst enemies are likely to be *your other bad habits*, so watch out for mutiny from within! Try to out-manoeuvre them with a brilliant counter-strategy or extra help from your allies or supporters.

For example:

- ask for a reminder call each day
- arrange a temporary loan
- clear the cupboards of biscuits and cakes
- empty the whiskey bottle down the sink
- find an assertive personal fitness trainer.

Devise Contingency Plans

Even the cleverest generals get it wrong sometimes, and the best-planned manoeuvres can fail simply because the enemy came up with the unexpected. So back up each strategy with an *alternative plan* which you can use in the event of a setback. Note down the numbers of any *rescue services* which could be of help, and make sure they are available for duty when and where you need them!

Your list might include, for example, the phone numbers of:

- supportive friends
- the leader of your self-help group
- a help-line
- your doctor

Keep Yourself in Tip-top Form

Doing battle with entrenched habits can, in the short term, be an enormous drain on your energy, so be careful not to become debilitated. Make sure your inner tank is continually fuelled with *nutritious food* and your battery is always fully charged. Of course you must not neglect your daily 'drills', but equally you need to make sure that you have adequate time to be *'at ease'*.

Maintain Your Appearance and Ship-shape Condition

Walk tall, shoulders back and head held high so you **look** *like a person who is fighting for self-respect*. Also, groom and dress yourself with utmost care so you *feel* *like a person you would want to defend* from a destructive habit!

Search Out the Heroes and Heroines

Listen (in person or through books, radio interviews or TV programmes) to your personal heroes' and heroines' *tales of triumph over enemies within*. But keep away from the shallow braggarts – and remember:

> *The really great make you feel that you too can become great.*
> MARK TWAIN

So choose your particular heroes and heroines carefully and then display their *photos, tips and words of wisdom* and any symbolic trophies you can get your hands on.

Be On Guard for 'Friendly' Predators

These are likely to come dressed in sheep's clothing. On the surface their intentions may seem caring and supportive, but their *'hidden agenda'* may be that they want to see you lose a battle which they themselves have never been able to win. For example, these envious predators often intervene with 'help' which they assure you is 'for your own good', for example:

- the friend who buys you one too many drinks ('Just because it's your birthday')
- the colleague who doesn't remind you of an important deadline ('Because you looked so tired.')
- the mother who teases you about your weight ('You're getting much too thin.').

Sharpen Up and Oil Your Weapons

Whatever weapons you choose, make sure they are sharp. For example, your self-protective assertive skills may need a polish (to ensure that you can say a firm 'no' or demand the best deal). (Consult the guidelines in Chapter 5.) Or alternatively, your sluggish brain may require a revitalizing shot of education to ensure that it is keen enough to leap to your defence.

Exploit Propaganda Techniques

Use empowering and motivational *self-talk*. Brainwash your mind with positive affirmations (see pages 70-72). For example:

'I am in control.'
'I am persistent.'
'I enjoy challenges.'
'I am a fighter and survivor.'
'I am a winner.'

Brag about your successes, but keep your setbacks a secret to all but your closest allies. During the battle, *ban association with the broadcasters of bad news.*

Reward and Honour Bravery

As the battle progresses, *ask for compliments* on your effort and exertion, especially in the disheartening early days when we often march forward one step and seem to take two steps back. Award yourself *mini-prizes* after the completion of almost every step in the advance. Celebrate each small victory and put on public display any examples of your success.

Expect to Meet Pain

Remind yourself *'no pain, no gain'*, but reassure yourself that in *this* war there will be *no fatalities* and its hurts will not only pass but be quickly forgotten in the glory of success! Work courageously through the pain barriers. If your wounds begin to get in the way of your progress, take some time at ease to rest and nurture yourself, but set a firm date for returning to the fray. During this time you could ask for some extra protection or help from a supportive ally, because this is the time when you are particularly vulnerable to enemy infiltration.

For example:

- if your muscles are aching and you decide to take break from the gym routine, you could ask a friend to check that you are at least still walking up the stairs and not taking the lift; to ward off the seduction of the cozy nights in front of the fire, arrange a date to meet at the gym in a week's time.

– if you are going to battle with your workaholism but have reached a point when your anxiety over your bulging in-tray is unbearable, take it home for *one* night. To ensure that old habits do not re-establish themselves, ask a colleague to lock it in the cupboard at the end of each day for the rest of the week!

Return to the fight *as soon as* you are revived and refreshed.

Take Regular Support from Comrades

Keep your kitbag of worries and fears *open and shared*. Allow yourself to be heartened by soothing consolations – and *frequent laughs* and sniggers at the enemies within!

Lay Plans for Victory Day

Keep these plans posted prominently to help encourage and motivate you.

Celebrate in Style

It's not enough to think that the end of the battle is reward enough. You and your self esteem should take advantage of every opportunity to *display your laurels* and enjoy the fruits of your hard-won success. *Public victory celebrations* can also be highly inspiring and motivating to others.

Keep Your Defences on Guard

Once the major battle is over, remember that it would be most unwise to give up your defensive position completely. In fact, with regard to certain enemy habits we must expect them to return again and again *throughout our lives*. The ones, for example, which were set in the impressionable years of early childhood are likely to re-emerge (sometimes with a vengeance) whenever we find ourselves under stress. So it is important to equip yourself with some information which will help your 'rear guard' do an effective job. You must have a clear idea of when, where and how the enemy is likely to reappear. One way of doing this is to make a list of the *'early warning signals'* which your defence team could use to stop a habit in its tracks before it takes hold again. For example, you could complete the following sentences (as many times as you like) and photocopy the finished list and pass it around to your supportive friends and colleagues – or you could insert a copy in your diary at the beginning of each month and use it as a checklist.

Please warn me when:

- I start to make excuses for not attending the...
- I start to talk about...
- I start to leave...
- I start to wear...
- I start to behave in a way which...
- I start to be...

The unfortunate thing about this world is that good habits are so much easier to give up than bad ones.

SOMERSET MAUGHAM

Yes, a good point, Mr Maugham, but you were writing before the Strategy for the Battle of the Bad Habits was won!

5

Strategies for Self-protection

Today's world is a dangerous place for self esteem. In Chapter 1 I listed many ways that, just in the course of our everyday lives as adults, we can come across all manner of destructive influences. Although overall I find our fast-moving competitive life very exciting and challenging, I also know that it can be very draining on my psychological reserves. I am sure you have had the experience of leaving the house one morning feeling like a giant, brimming with self-confidence and self-love and then returning the same evening feeling more like an insignificant, depressed ant! This metamorphosis may have taken place simply because during the course of one not-too-extraordinary day you encountered an unexpected surfeit of disappointment, stress and insensitivity.

The optimist in me is convinced that the more widespread the 'gospel' of personal development becomes, the less destructive of human self esteem society will be. But even my vision of this paradise (where self-worth and confidence are continually boosted and enhanced) is still very faint, and I have no doubt that those of us with fragile inner resources will need high-quality self-protective skills for very many years to come.

I have found that there are three main areas of personal

development work which have proved to be especially useful to people who want to strengthen their 'defenses' against hostile external influences. These are:

1. Positive thinking
2. Assertiveness
3. Stress management.

In this chapter I intend to discuss each of these briefly in turn, and then introduce a selection of appropriate strategies and techniques. Those of you who are familiar with my earlier books may find that some of this material provokes *déjà vu*, but I am hoping that, even if it does, it can still be useful as a stimulating refresher course. My explanations for the 'old' strategies have been rewritten and the examples are new and all relevant to self esteem building. Alternatively, you could of course move on to the next chapter, but before doing so may I suggest that at the very least you skim through the headings to make sure that you are fully conversant with each technique and you are not missing out on any new gems!

In contrast, those of you who are new to any of these subjects may want to supplement your reading of this chapter with other books, because you could find some of my explanations frustratingly short! If you do, I suggest that you consult the Further Reading chapter (pages 191-2) and obtain a more detailed book on the subject before moving on to begin the practical work in Section Three.

Positive Thinking

Over the past few years the personal development market has become flooded with books and courses on positive thinking. The irony is that, in the main, these books are still being sought and bought by people who probably *need* them least!

Until relatively recently they have only attracted the attention of enterprising, ambitious people who have already achieved a fair amount of success in the world of business and sport, who (perhaps because they have good self esteem!) want to have even more.

But it is of course people with rocky, low self esteem who need, more than anyone else, to reprogramme themselves to think more positively. After all, not only do they carry around a subconscious that is deeply impregnated with negative beliefs and attitudes, but they also have an entrenched habit of attracting new reinforcing negative experiences. For example, they are much more likely than most to:

- feel 'at home' surrounded by friends and family who delight in swapping 'Isn't it awful?' stories and pouring scorn and cynicism on aspiring optimists and achievers ('You'll soon realize...nothing lasts for ever...life wasn't meant to be easy...life is just as awful if you have money or success,' etc.)
- soak up words of 'wisdom' from pessimists about their potential because these feel like 'the truth' and fit in neatly with the negative messages they already have about themselves. They readily listen when people say 'It'll be too hard for you,' or 'Don't you try, you'll only make a mess of it' and they won't even hear the words of the encouragers telling them to 'Go for it.'
- find themselves attracted to the satirical novel, the great tragedies and funereal music, and may genuinely judge comedies and romantic tales to be insubstantial and boring
- be working in situations where there is no shortage of inequality and discrimination, where people constantly moan about the unfairness and hopeless- ness of it all
- be sought out by people in BIG TROUBLE (because they are so 'nice' and need to continue be seen so!).

You will have already gathered that I do not believe that the 'quick fix' approach (which characterizes so many schools of Positive Thinking) can *alone* counter such ingrained negative habits, although some of the techniques can be exceedingly helpful when they are integrated into other programmes. I have therefore selected four simple strategies which I will be suggesting you use in the programmes in Section Three. But you will have nothing to lose if you want to put them to a more immediate test!

The first, called GEE STRATEGY, is my own and you will find a further explanation and more examples in one of my earlier books, *The Positive Woman* (Thorsons, 1992). The other three (Reframing, Affirmations, and Anchoring) are well-known positive thinking techniques which I have adapted slightly to suit our self esteem building purpose.

The GEE Strategy

When you find yourself feeling negatively inclined towards yourself, another person, an opportunity, a problem or even the day itself, use this strategy to check whether or not your thoughts are rational or irrational.

First, ask yourself these three simple questions. If your answer to any of them is 'Yes,' then restate your thought more positively and rationally.

1. Am I GENERALIZING from a specific experience?:

    a) 'Last time I tried this it was a disaster; don't give it to me to do I'm bound to mess it up.'
        → 'I didn't do this very well last time, but the chances are that I will have learned from that mistake and will do it better this time.'
    b) 'ALL female bosses are "stand-offish" (because that is how Moira was).'
        → 'Some female bosses can be very approachable.'

2. Am I EXAGGERATING current problems or potential hazards or difficulties?:

   a) 'I'm a walking disaster when it comes to decorating.'
      →'I have made several bad mistakes when decorating. It's not one of my best skills.'
   b) 'This is an IMPOSSIBLE task.'
      →'This is a challenging task.'

3. Am I EXCLUDING any positive aspects or potential?:

   a) 'There's no point in me applying for that job, they'll think I'm too old.'
      → 'My chances are not great for this particular job, but they may be the kind of organization that needs people with experience. I have nothing to lose from trying.'
   b) 'This is a TOTALLY disastrous development.'
      → 'This development will present us with many opportunities to test and improve our team work.'

Reframing

This simple technique can be used to turn a statement or question with a negative frame of reference into one which has a more positive tone. It can be used as a form of self-protection when you are in the company of negative thinkers, especially those who are likely to feed on any self-criticism or worry you might share. You can see from these examples how just by reframing your opening sentence you can help yourself think more positively while at the same time setting a brighter tone to a conversational exchange and so lessening the chance of being loaded with put-downs and moans.

Examples

a) 'I'm afraid this report is on the short side.'
→ 'You'll be pleased to hear this report is concise and to the point.'

b) 'It's nerve-wracking, isn't it, with so many new people here? It'll be so difficult to bring up the subject – you never know what to say, you could so easily offend someone.'
→ 'It's exciting to see so many new people here – there must be so many different viewpoints represented, I shall find it quite an interesting challenge to find the right way to bring up the subject.'

c) 'I know I look dreadful in green, you're always telling me I shouldn't wear it but it was such a bargain that I'm afraid I used up all the money anyway because I couldn't resist these shoes.'
→ 'I'm really proud of myself for finding such a bargain and even though it isn't my best colour the design suits me and I had enough money over to buy some wonderful shoes as well.'

d) 'It's very nosy of me to ask, but why do you look so miserable?'
→ 'I appreciate that you might find my curiosity intrusive, but I thought you looked sad and I just wondered if talking to me might help. I am a good listener.'

e) 'What a queue! It's going to drive me mad standing here wasting my time. Isn't it dreadful?'
→ 'This is a long queue – at least I will have 10 minutes of uninterrupted time to 'switch off'/sort out my thoughts for.../have an interesting chat,' etc.

Affirmations

These are positive statements which we say to ourselves on a regular basis. They are especially useful in helping us to take control over the negative conditioning we may have received in our early years, and which has most probably been heavily reinforced since then. They can also be used to bolster us up when we know we are going into difficult situations or are going to spend time in the company of people who are likely to make us feel either 'small' or depressed – or both!

Many people find that affirmations are most effective when they use the *first-person* ('I') and the *present tense* (as in my examples below), but I have also found that future tense ('I will do it'/'I will enjoy it') and more general statements ('Life is exciting'/'Work can be fun as well as necessary') are also very useful. I believe (but again, others disagree!) that it is important to use statements which are *realistic* and not 'over-the-top' (e.g. *not* 'I'm *the greatest!* I can achieve *anything*').

When saying affirmations, speak them aloud whenever possible, while using an appropriately positive and assertive tone. Relax and smile as you are speaking. Often people say them aloud routinely when they are alone (e.g. getting ready for work in the morning). If you do this, you will find that the affirmations are more likely to leap easily to mind when you need a boost of silent positive self-talk in a difficult or depressing situation.

General examples which you can say repeatedly to yourself:

I am a positive person.
I enjoy challenges.
I am a good organizer.
I am an excellent mother/father/son etc.
I make my work interesting and stimulating.
I am creative in my approach to problem solving.
I take care to maintain my relationships.

Examples of affirmations you can say to yourself when you find you are in difficult circumstances and company and want to protect your self esteem:

I choose to be an optimist.
I can take control of my feelings.
I am learning from this experience.
I am the best judge of my own values.

I decide what can hurt my feelings and what will not.
I accept that other people are different from me.
I choose my friends.
I enjoy the world with all its imperfections.

Anchoring

This technique enables us to utilize positive experiences from our past to 'fuel' us when we may need an extra boost of confidence or positivity. It involves programming our brain to associate the positive feelings of the past experience with a particular thought, word or physical sensation or movement (or with all three). We are then able to recall the positive emotional feelings whenever we choose to think of that occasion, use our 'trigger word' and/or enact the associated physical movement.

Self-help Method

Use your favourite relaxation technique to get yourself into a *deeply* relaxed ('floating' but still conscious!) state. Recall, in as much vivid detail as possible, an experience from the past which helped you feel that your self esteem was particularly strong. Use your imagination to 're-live' the experience slowly and fully, physically and emotionally. Try to recapture the memory of the sensations you felt in your body, including the kind of scents you could smell and the sounds you could hear.

With your mind's eye, spend a few minutes looking at yourself enjoying this experience – while at the same time saying a particular word and/or making a movement (e.g. tapping your finger on, or lightly squeezing a part of your body.) This 'trigger' movement should be small (and discreet!) so that will be able to do it in public without anyone noticing.

Repeat the above on several occasions – until you find that you are able to respond automatically with your positive high self esteem feeling when you conjure up your picture in your imagination, say your word, and/or feel your physical trigger.

Experiment, as soon as possible, with using this anchor in real-life situations. The more often you use the anchor, the more powerful and useful it will be.

Assertiveness

Well-exercised assertive skills not only help us to be more positive and direct in asking for our needs to be met, they also can play an invaluable role in protecting our self-worth and confidence. When we are being assertive we both feel, and look, cool, calm and collected. Even if we do not get what we want, we emerge from situations with our self-respect intact, knowing that we have behaved honourably and with dignity. If we happen to be disappointed with the outcome we do not come away kicking ourselves for being a 'wimp' or 'bully', we admire ourselves for having the courage to try and the dignity to remain in control. Furthermore, people who are witness to our assertive behaviour are usually similarly impressed and much more likely to treat us with respect and consideration.

What Is Assertive Behaviour?

Assertiveness is still commonly confused in our society with aggressiveness, but I believe that their styles are different in two very crucial respects. Aggression is often used by people who are determined to 1) *get what they want and* 2) *get it at the expense of other people*. Assertiveness, on the other hand, is about 1) *aiming and asking for what you want* (in the full knowledge that you might not be successful), using behaviours which are always 2) *respectful of the rights of other people*.

The following adjectives are ones which I commonly use to describe people whose behaviour is consistently assertive:

- direct and open
- clear and concise
- persistent and firm
- relaxed and controlled
- positive and lively
- innovative and challenging
- co-operative and democratic
- self-protective and self-nurturing
- fair and just.

If you are beginning to go green with envy for these paragons, you may be comforted to know that there are sometimes important advantages to using the other two main alternatives: 'fight' style (aggression) and 'flight' style (passivity). In fact, I believe that this is especially so for people with low self esteem, who tend to attract *an above-average amount of discrimination and abuse.* You may therefore find that, until your self esteem improves, it is in your interests to use these latter two styles much more frequently than a super-confident person would use them. Be patient with yourself and don't make matters worse by criticizing yourself for not being as assertive as you would like to be.

Unfortunately I can give you no definitive guidelines about when and where each of the three styles of behaviour should be used, because ultimately such decisions have to be personal ones. They must always take into account *your own morality, needs and goals* and be selected according to their *appropriateness* for each situation.

Having given these rather solemn warnings, I am pleased to be able move on to the good news! There are five important strategies and techniques that we use in Assertiveness Training which I am confident will be very useful and self-protective, not only as you work through the programmes in this book but also when you have reached the dizzy heights of super-confidence. They are:

1. Broken Record
2. Fogging
3. Negative Assertion
4. Negative Enquiry
5. Scripting.

I suggest that, after you have read through the descriptions of the five strategies, you learn and practise using each one in the company of a friend or a self-help group. Through experimenting with role-play you will soon become convinced of the protective qualities of these techniques and you will find out how to adapt them to suit your own language and situations. After some rehearsal the strategies will begin to feel less like artificial techniques and more like your 'normal' everyday behaviour. Eventually you will even find yourself using them spontaneously and confidently.

If it is difficult for you to role-play, write down as many variations of each strategy as you can think of, then say them aloud using a strong, clear tone of voice. If you record and listen to yourself several times you will imprint the new responses in your subconscious mind and your confidence will be boosted as you hear yourself sounding so much more assertive. (Don't forget to reward yourself each time!).

Just before I introduce each of the five strategies, I want to put on my warning hat again and make the following points!

1. It is rarely a good idea to use any of the following strategies in emergency situations where anyone's physical safety (or perhaps livelihood) is in jeopardy. On those occasions passive (flight) or aggressive (fight) responses are more likely to be the most protective.
2. The main function of the first three strategies, in particular, is to protect you by stopping the 'offender' in his or her tracks. They are *not* designed to make either you or the other person more likeable or lovable, and should not be relied upon to resolve complicated and important relationship or moral issues.
3. Each strategy should only be used when you are convinced of your moral or legal right to protect yourself or make your request.
4. You should always calm yourself down before speaking and ensure that you are using assertive body language. Remember that although sometimes it is appropriate to use a relaxed smile, your overall tone should be serious and you should look relaxed and in control.

Broken Record

Outline of Strategy

You *state directly and concisely* either:

- what you want or need or feel
- what you are prepared to do, or not to do
- what you would like the other person to do, or stop doing

Continually *repeat a one-sentence summary* of this message over and over again until the person concerned either 'gives in' or you both agree on a reasonable compromise.

When to Use It

It is particularly useful as a self-protective aid when:

- your *moral or human legal rights are being abused* and you want immediate justice (e.g. disrespectful behaviour or poor service or shoddy goods)
- you wish to *preserve your time or energy* and do not want to be sidetracked into argument (e.g. being 'baited' before an important meeting)
- you want to *persist in your refusal to assume unfair responsibilities* (e.g. working too much overtime or looking after children too much of the time)
- you wish to *affirm your right to postpone dealing with a problem* because it is not your current priority (e.g. when you are too tired or too busy to discuss it)
- you need to *emphasize an important point and are not being listened to attentively* (e.g. being continually interrupted in a meeting or when trying to declare 'Bedtime!' against the background of TV)
- something requires *urgent attention or immediate action and you cannot afford to be 'fobbed off'* (e.g. a letter must reach *today's* post or your pain is excruciating and you need a doctor *now*)

- you may wish to *affirm your right to a certain feeling* in the face of someone telling you that you ought to be experiencing a different emotion (e.g. feeling too afraid to dive in when someone else laughs and says 'you can't be frightened', or being pleased with grade B when someone else thinks you should be ashamed for not getting an A).

How to Use It

Compose your concise Broken Record sentence, being careful to ensure that your demands are realistic and legally and morally justified. It is preferable to start with 'I/We would...' or 'Would you..' You can, of course, insert the word 'please', but you will probably have more impact if it does not begin the sentence.

Compose an additional sentence which indicates that you have considered the feelings, position or predicament of the other person (e.g. 'I understand that it is difficult for you, but...' / 'I can see that you're upset, but...'). This expression of empathy will increase your chances of being listened to attentively and sympathetically.

Using a calm, strong, clear tone of voice, repeat the first sentence over and over again while occasionally inserting an expression of empathy if and when it is appropriate to do so. Use your first sentence as your *key* response to anything that the other party might say (either verbally or non-verbally). Do not argue back to any excuses, put-downs, threats or emotional blackmail which you might receive – simply persist with your 'Broken Record'.

Example A
(Note that the Broken Record is in *italics* and the empathy statement is in **bold**)

John: Could you do the agenda for tomorrow's meeting before you leave tonight?

Tony: *I can't work overtime tonight*, I'm sorry I have an important commitment.

John: Well, the agenda must be done or the meeting will be a shambles.

Tony: **I appreciate that it's going to be difficult** but *I can't work overtime tonight.*

John: It would take you no more than half an hour.

Tony: *I can't work overtime tonight*, I have an important commitment.

John: There's no way I can do it – can't you do me this one favour? After all, I helped you with the spreadsheet last week.

Tony: **I know it's a problem for you**, but *I can't work overtime tonight.*

John: I suppose we'll have to muddle through, then.

Example B

Linda: *I'd like you to call me Linda*, not 'luvvy'

Richard: What's eating you today – had a rough night last night?

Linda : I just said *I'd like you to call me Linda.*

Richard: It's just an expression – I'm not trying to patronize or seduce you. We don't like too much formality round here – perhaps it was different in your last office.

Linda: **I guess it might sound a bit formal to you**, but *I'd like you to call me Linda.*

Richard: All right, have it your way. Linda, would you mind...?

Fogging

Outline of Strategy

You respond to unwanted criticism by using a reply which implies that there *may* be a *probability* that the critic *could* be right, even though inwardly you may know or think he or she is completely wrong. The critic is usually taken aback because he or she does not get the response intended and is not sure what is going on (hence the name of this one, 'fogging').

You continue to 'fog' each additional criticism until the critic gives up when he or she realizes that there is no satisfaction to be had in attacking this victim!

When to Use It

It can be used whenever you are being criticized:

- by someone whom you consider has no right to criticize you
- at an inconvenient time or in an inappropriate setting (and you may want to postpone dealing with the criticism)
- before you have had time to calm down and think through an assertive reply
- by someone whose good opinion isn't needed by you and you want to preserve your energy and time
- and your critic is loading you with insults and put-downs which are so 'irrational' that it is pointless for you to engage in serious debate
- by someone who is angry and you want to wait until he or she is calmer before tackling the criticism
- and you feel yourself getting tearful or angry and want to postpone discussion until you feel more in control of your feelings

N.B. At first glance this technique may look more like a people-pleasing habit rather than a self esteem boosting skill, but I can assure you that when it is used consciously and appropriately as a self-defence mechanism it is an *invaluable* boost to our personal power.

Example A
(Fogged responses are in *italics*)

Impatient bus driver: You ought to have had the fare ready – we can't wait all day while you fumble in your purse.

Out-of breath mother: *Maybe I am a bit slow –*

Bus driver: If you're going to bring kids on a bus you should be better organized.

Mother: *Perhaps you're right*. One and two halves to the church, please.

Example B

Angry colleague: You stupid idiot – why did you leave the samples there? You can't be trusted with anything. You're a...

Semi-guilty colleague: *Perhaps it wasn't the best place to put them*.

Angry colleague: If I were in charge here I'd have you sacked immediately! People like you just cause trouble – wherever you are there's chaos.

Semi-guilty colleague: *Maybe I'm not the easiest person to work with*.

Angry colleague: I don't know why that idiot thinks people with a load of paper qualifications are fit to run a warehouse.

Semi-guilty colleague: *You could be right*, perhaps I haven't enough practical experience.

Angry colleague: Well, let's forget it this time but I hope you'll think before you act next time.

Semi-guilty colleague: I will.

Negative Assertion

Outline of Strategy

You respond to the critic by *calmly agreeing with the truth, or element of truth*, in what he or she is saying without adding a defensive justification which could fuel an argument. You use the strategy until the other person gives up the 'attack'.

When to Use It

Use this technique only when *you are sure that you do agree* (use

Fogging if you do not). Even though your critic may have hit 'an Achilles' heel' you may still want to stop the flow of criticisms because:

- you are being criticized for a fault or mistake which you have already taken on board and are working on to correct
- you are being criticized for a 'fault' such as a physical defect or genetic characteristic which you cannot change but do not (for whatever reason) want to defend at this moment (or ever)
- you are hearing the same old story and do not want to have to waste energy justifying yourself again and again
- your critic has chosen an inopportune or insensitive time to remind you of your faults or mistakes
- you are too busy or tired to deal with your critic and would prefer to discuss the matter later
- your critic (however right) is not the kind of person with whom you want to explore your weaknesses.

In the following examples note how using this technique helps to keep the scenes from escalating into unwanted arguments.

Example A

Mother: You're always too busy. You never seem to have time to talk to me when I ring.

Jill: *Yes it's true, I don't often have time to talk to you when you ring these days.*

Mother: You ought to take better care of yourself – you work too many evenings.

Jill: *Yes, you're right I am working too many evenings at the moment.*

Mother: The children must get fed up as well – they can't be seeing enough of you.

Jill: *I know they are not seeing enough of me at the moment.*

Mother: Well I hope things will be different next week. I'll ring you again then.

Jill: Thanks – I'll look forward to a long chat then.

Example B

Simon: You're late again.

Jackie: *Yes, I'm late.*

Simon: It's getting to be a really bad habit.

Jackie: *It is a bad habit.*

Simon: You're full of bad habits you are.

Jackie: *Yes. I'm certainly not perfect.*

Simon: You ought to sort yourself out – you'll never get on in this place if you don't.

Jackie: *It's true I do need to change in several ways.*

Simon: Women are all the same – they never take their work seriously enough. Home is where their heart is, they'll never change.

Jackie: *I do put a high value on my personal life.*

Simon: Well I suppose it's your life – if you want it that way. But don't moan about not having enough money.

Jackie: No I won't.

Negative Enquiry

Outline of Strategy

You respond to the critic's verbal or non-verbal indication of disapproval by asking for *clarification* or directly *inviting criticism*. If the critic should then launch into unwanted criticism you can stop his or her flow by using Fogging or Negative Assertion as above. If the criticism is valid and useful, you can (if you have the time and energy) continue to use the strategy to gain more specific information.

When to Use It

You can use this strategy when:

• you are puzzled by a remark or 'look' and think that it may

indicate an unwarranted, unfair or ill-timed criticism
- you are not sure whether the critic is well-intentioned and is simply asking for information/trying to give you helpful feedback or is in fact trying to 'bait' you (because perhaps you're seen as an easy target, or because your critic is simply bored)
- you think someone might be 'backbiting' or gossiping about you, and you want to expose and stop the source

Warning! Be careful only to use Negative Enquiry when your self esteem feels relatively resilient and you feel confident enough to use either Fogging or Negative Assertion to block further criticism.

In the following examples the Negative Enquiry is in *italics* and any subsequent Fogging or Negative Assertion statement is **bold**.

Example A

Anthony: How come you arrived here before anyone else?

Roger: *Are you saying that you think I was driving too fast?*

Anthony: You're so competitive, you have to win at everything.

Roger: **Perhaps I do like winning**.

Example B

Sheila: When I came in the room, the conversation went dead. Were you talking about me? As this has happened several times this week *I was wondering whether I am doing anything you don't like or may disapprove of?*

Robert: Well, yes, we do think you've become a bit bossy lately.

Sheila: *In what ways? Can you give me an example?*

Robert: It's just your attitude.

Sheila: *Do you think that I don't care about your feelings?*

Robert: No, it isn't that. It's just that since you've been promoted you're no fun any more.

Sheila: **Perhaps I am a bit serious**, but in future if you want to make comments about my style of management I

would prefer you to do so to my face, and not choose a time when we are trying to prepare for an important meeting.

Scripting

Outline of Strategy

You use a set structure and strict guidelines to help you prepare a concise assertive opening 'speech' and then thoroughly rehearse it (in your head, out loud or in role-play). Your prepared script helps you to sound so authoritative and confident that you are usually listened to with attention and respect; your chances of getting what you want or need are therefore greatly increased.

When to Use It

You can use this strategy when you want to make almost any request or a justified complaint, but it is particularly useful when:

- you know that you are likely to be more passive or aggressive than you would like to be
- your feelings of anxiety or frustration may need to be kept under good control
- you know you will be speaking to someone who may not give you the attention you deserve because he or she is busy or very preoccupied
- the person you will be talking to is intimidating or might pre-judge you as 'wimpish' or your needs as unimportant
- you want to follow up a criticism which you had previously blocked with Fogging or Negative Assertion
- you want to set a positive, upbeat tone to a negotiation process (especially useful when the other party is highly defensive or pessimistic).

Although Scripting is most commonly used to prepare for verbal encounters, it can also be used as an invaluable guide for composing punchy, concise letters or short reports or requisitions. In fact, when people with low self esteem first start using assertiveness, written complaints and requests (even to intimate friends and family) may be the most self-protective option, and should certainly not be regarded as cowardly 'cop-outs'.

How to Prepare a Script

I have used the following mnemonic sentence as a reminder of the four major components of a script: Explanation, Feelings, Needs, and Consequences. It is important that each is addressed – and for maximum impact, in the order which I suggest.

86

Even	Fish	Need	Confidence
X	E	E	O
P	E	E	N
L	L	D	S
A	I	S	E
N	N		Q
A	G		U
T	S		E
I			N
O			C
N			E
			S

Explanation

Explain the situation objectively and concisely, using only one sentence whenever possible. Do not include justifications or theories about the 'whys' and 'wherefores' of the situation.

Feelings

Share your own feelings accurately, using an assertive 'I feel...' statement rather than an accusatory 'You (or it) makes me feel...'

Briefly indicate that you have considered the other person's feelings or predicament (your empathy statement).

Needs

Say directly and concisely what it is you want or do not want, but ensure your requests are realistic. If your requests number more than one or two or are quite complicated to explain, make a general request at this stage such as asking for a further discussion or that your written report be given priority attention. If a compromise is appropriate, include a statement which suggests that you are willing to negotiate.

Consequences

Spell out the 'pay-off' there will be for the other person should he or she comply with your wishes or listen to your 'case' sympathetically and attentively.

In brackets after writing your script, note down the negative consequences you could use to 'threaten' or 'punish' the other person should he or she not respond to your request. Then decide whether the carrot (positive consequences) or stick (negative consequences) is more justified. Although you may never have to resort to using your 'negative consequences' (Scripting is so effective!), just noting them down boosts your sense of personal power.

Example A
'Yesterday you began to criticize me when we were standing in the queue at the station (**Explanation**). I felt embarrassed and cross with you (**Your feelings**), and although I know that you had good grounds for complaint (**empathy with their feelings**), I would like you to choose a less public place in which to confront me (**your needs**) – that way I'll be much more likely to take on board what you are trying to tell me (**positive consequences**).'

or

' – otherwise I will not feel like doing what you want and will be far less likely to change (**negative consequences**).'

Example B
'I have only left the office once on time over the last three weeks, and now at the last minute you have again presented me with urgent work in spite of my request to leave on time today (**Explanation**). I am beginning to feel quite annoyed (**Feelings**), and though I know that this is a very special order for you (**empathy**) I would like you, on this occasion, to give it to someone else to do or leave it until the morning (**needs**) as a) it will be done much more efficiently if it is not a rushed job and b) you will not feel guilty for causing me to miss my train again tonight! (**positive consequences**)'

or

– '...a) I will feel less and less willing to do overtime and b) I will start job-hunting! (**negative consequences**)'

Stress Management

Nowadays nearly everyone I meet professes to be some kind of amateur expert on stress management. If I am looking weary and harassed I find no shortage of inspiring tips and sound advice. And of course there are also the 'real' experts. They appear to be sprouting forth in their hundreds from a whole new set of industries and professions responding to the needs of our fast-paced, highly pressurized society. So, not wanting to feel left out, I thought that I'd throw in a few ideas here as well!

Seriously, though, *active* stress management must always be a very important part of both building and preserving your self esteem. If you think your ways of coping with pressure are still inadequate, I would suggest that you take some time out to make use of the many available courses, or to read one of the variety of books now on the market. In the mean time, here are a few guidelines and some techniques which I have found particularly relevant and helpful. You could use the following list as a checklist once a month or when you know you are working under a considerable amount of pressure.

GENERAL TIPS FOR MANAGING STRESS
WHEN UNDER PRESSURE

- Prioritize tasks and plan a timetable at the start of each day.
- Take regular short breaks throughout the day. Use one of the 'quick-fix' relaxers below, or just stretch out and breathe deeply and calmly for at least two to three minutes every hour.
- Keep a watchful eye on your posture and regularly check that you are not holding yourself in tense positions and that your body is well supported.
- Eat healthy foods which stimulate your palette as well as your intestines! Have a selection of these always readily

available. Set yourself a limit on the amount of stimulants and toxins (such as caffeine and alcohol) you will allow yourself each day.

- Go to bed at least 30 minutes before you usually do, and get up 15 minutes earlier than you strictly need to. Establish stimulating morning and calming evening rituals to do each day.
- De-stress your environment as much as possible (e.g. make sure your workspace and your home have excellent lighting, supportive seating and low noise levels, and that they are tidy!)
- Make regular appointments in your diary to talk to and share with good listeners who care about you and the issues which are of concern to you.
- Release cathartically any pent-up emotions as soon as it is appropriate for you to do so – find a private space where you can laugh/cry/growl/scream/thump a cushion/beat a drum, etc. Or start playing a sport or doing a hobby which allows you to release pent-up frustrations.
- Give your mind at least two 'switch off' periods each day – one using your favourite music, books or TV programme, one using 'clearing' techniques such as meditation or one of the 'quick-fixes' below.
- Engage in at least 10 – 15 minutes of moderate physical exercise each day, and three 20-minute sessions of more rigorous exercise every week.
- Use *deep*-relaxation techniques for at least 20 minutes once a week (e.g. a relaxation tape, sauna, massage or just a prolonged aromatherapy bath by candlelight).
- Plan periods for fun activities into your timetable at the start of each week to stimulate your humour and spontaneity.

'Quick-Fix' Relaxers

Mini-Physical Workout

When to Use

Anytime when you feel your physical tension stopping you from feeling or looking as relaxed as you need or want to be. Use it as soon as you notice the butterflies in your stomach, the feeling of heaviness in your head or that tell-tale stiffness in your neck. Also try to get into the habit of doing it routinely before entering any potentially nerve-wracking situation, such as giving a presentation, meeting a difficult customer or even joining the family Christmas party!

- Find a quiet corner where there are no prying, quizzical eyes (the loo will do!). First, gently move your head from side to side and then up and down to release any tension in your neck. Tightly screw up your face and tense up as much of your body, hold for a couple of seconds and then *slowly* let your muscles relax. Repeat several times, ending with two full body stretches. Give your wrists and ankles a good shake; rotate your shoulders in both directions and up and down; then swing the top half of your body around on your hips several times. Finally after giving yourself a thorough shake, take a few slow deep breaths and repeat three times to yourself 'I am relaxed' – and then return to the fray!
- If you cannot leave the room (perhaps because you are sitting around a conference or dining table), you can relax yourself by consciously unwinding your body (e.g. uncrossing your legs, dropping your shoulders, sitting up straight so that your body is more supported). Secretly (perhaps under the table!) clench one or both of your fists and then slowly relax them. Repeat the same process with your feet and toes. No one will notice, but you will immediately feel more relaxed and in control, and you can be assured that when you speak your voice will project with more volume and impact because you are relaxed.

Magic Mental Reviver

Where to Use

This technique can be used literally anywhere, such as standing in a queue at a supermarket or sitting outside an interview or exam room, but it works even better if you can find somewhere to lie down or sit in a Lotus-style position.

- Close your eyes. Consciously relax any tension in your body. Check that your face, jaw, hands, arms, legs and feet are loose, and consciously allow yourself to sink into, and feel supported by, whatever surface you are sitting or lying on.
- Take three or four slow deep breaths, while mentally following the passage of your breath as it goes in and out (sometimes it helps to imagine it as one colour as it is drawn in and another as it is expelled).
- Now let yourself breathe naturally and easily, while slowly counting backwards from 50 or simply saying the alphabet.
- Finish with a few moments of allowing your mind just to float gently.
- Repeat, if you have time.

Positive Affirmation Meditation

- Relax yourself as in either (or both) of the exercises above.
- With your eyes closed, say a very short appropriate affirmation sentence as you breathe in and out (e.g. while breathing in: 'I am...;' as you breathe out: '...confident/in control/likeable/courageous/peaceful,' etc.).
- As thoughts, worries or ruminations come to mind, gently return your focus to your affirmation sentence.

Scenic Symbol Meditation

- Relax yourself, again as above.
- Close your eyes and focus your mind's eye on a chosen symbol or scene which conjures up feelings of peace and relaxation (e.g. a favourite room, sunset on the beach, a sleeping cat, a sunflower, etc.).
- Use your imagination to examine your symbol in minute detail. Every time a thought comes into your head, refocus your mind's eye on your symbol.

'The Night Before' Pacifier

Creative Visualization

This creative visualization technique uses your imagination to help you rehearse your confidence skills and feed your subconscious an image of you successfully achieving your goal with the minimum amount of stress.

When to Use It
The evening before you have to face a difficult challenge, when you need to feel both confident and relaxed. The exercise will take between 20 minutes and one hour, depending on how much time you can spare (the longer the better!). You could have some gently relaxing music on in the background.

- Lie in a place where you can be private and undisturbed (the bath?) and spend about 10 minutes relaxing your body to the stage where your mind has reached that wonderful 'floating' level.
- Staying relaxed and breathing rhythmically and gently, take your imagination to the time when you are due to wake up the next morning. Visualize yourself getting dressed and generally preparing for your day in a very

easy-going way. See yourself enjoying a nurturing, relaxed breakfast.

- Continue to visualize yourself going through the events of your day in a very positive, relaxed frame of mind. Take care to get a picture of yourself looking cool, calm and collected through any crisis or difficult time which you anticipate you might have. Notice the details – especially your body language – and try to hear in your mind's ear the confident, controlled tones of your voice. Admire your vision of the relaxed 'you' for as long as you can, because the stronger this image is the more likely it is to become reality tomorrow!

Time Management Spot-check

- Each morning after you have made your prioritized list of 'things to do today' (you do, don't you?!), review it and give each item a 'Stress factor' mark on a scale of 1 – 10.
- According to the level of stress you have assessed, add an

appropriate relaxation activity.
- When you review your list at the end of the day, note whether a) you have given yourself your 'stress-busting' activity and b) whether it was effective. If you find that your efforts consistently fall below your required standards, try pinning up a note of your resolution to relax daily in a public place, and ask to be gently reminded about it!

Stress Symptom Monitor

When to Use

Preferably *every* week!

- Make a short checklist of your own special symptoms which indicate that you may be experiencing too much stress (or photocopy the one in the list below, remembering that this list is not exhaustive).
- Get a number of photocopies of your list so that you can use one for the end of each week or, at the very least, at the end of each month. Put them in your stress management or personal development file (you did start one, didn't you?!).
- Mark yourself on a scale of 1 – 10 according to how well you are managing your stress.

SYMPTOMS WHICH COMMONLY INDICATE
TOO MUCH STRESS

Physical Symptoms
indigestion
tension headaches
blocked sinuses
bowel problems – diarrhoea or constipation

frequent urination
shoulder, back or neck ache
skin rashes
stiffness in joints
frequent 'pins and needles'
dizziness
excessive PMT

Emotional Symptoms

tearfulness
irritability
anxiety attacks
uncontrollable worrying
increase in lack of confidence
increase in obsessions or phobias
palpitations
over-excitability
lack of excitability or passion
feelings of confusion
a feeling of being overwhelmed
apathy
a feeling of powerlessness
depersonalization (a feeling of watching the world from the outside)
loss of trust in people – increased cynicism

Behavioural Symptoms

poor concentration
inability to listen attentively
talking too much
inability to control giggling fits, nervous tics, etc.
talking too little – going quiet
being reclusive, e.g. always lunching alone
rushing around
shouting more than usual
clumsiness
nervous habits e.g. nail-biting, scratching, picking
difficulty making decisions

poor planning leading to too-tight schedules
reluctance to delegate
making 'mountains out of molehills'
unkempt appearance
missing exercise workouts or sport schedules
not spending time on hobbies
an empty social diary
being over-protective
playing it 'too safe' – not taking usual calculated risks
over-spending and mounting debt
getting up or going to bed too late
insomnia
nightmares
forgetting more than usual
missing appointments, birthdays, etc.

Section 3
Self-Help Programmes

Section One hopefully fuelled you with motivation to acquire the unquestionable advantages of high self esteem; Section Two provided you with some of the essential fundamental tools. Now Section Three is going to show you the way to get into action. The next three chapters contain a series of practical self-help programmes which I have designed to help you look after your own self esteem so that you can depend on it to remain in a consistently healthy condition for evermore.

So, say a final good-bye to your excuses and wishful thinking and brace yourself for empowering action!

Have you ever imagined how wonderful it must be to live the privileged life of a well-loved and meticulously maintained vintage car? I doubt it, but if you've read this far I am banking on the fact that you might be 'game to try'!

As in my earlier chapter on breaking self-destructive habits, throughout this section I will be using a loose metaphor to bring alive my suggested strategies for boosting your self esteem and maintaining it in good order. Once again I have chosen to use a subject (car maintenance!) which I know virtually nothing about, so I must beg mercy and patience from enthusiasts and professionals in this field. I feel sure that some of my analogies will not stand the test of rigorous analysis by competent mechanics, but hopefully they will make sense to lesser mortals and will serve their purpose as light-hearted memory aids.

In Chapter 6 you will be working through a programme of exercises which will help you to give your special 'car' a thorough transformation. You will be giving it a first-class recondition and then treat it to the kind of valeting service which is normally reserved for the Rolls Royces of the motoring world. Once its engine has begun to 'purr' again and it is gleaming with showroom shine, by following the guidelines in Chapters 7 and 8 you will then be able to promise it a guarantee of regular maintenance and respectful driving! (Remember this is a truly 'green' fantasy – there's no room for premature write-offs and glossy new-car brochures!)

Before starting the next chapter, you will need to spend a few moments selecting a particular second-hand car to represent you and your self esteem. Choose a model which feels appropriate to your personality and lifestyle. You could be a creaky vintage veteran, a worthy but well-worn family saloon or a speedily disintegrating sports special! It does not matter how much wear and tear you may be currently showing or feeling, just as long as you know that underneath your scratches and grime there lurks potential!

Now, stop reading and choose your car!

6

The Big Recondition

*A 12-step Programme Designed to Give You and Your
self esteem a Major Overhaul and a Psychological Boost*

Step 1: Display an Inspirational 'Show-model'

Before beginning to strip down the engine or bodywork of any car, I am sure that competent mechanics must have a clear picture in their heads of what a similar model in tip-top condition both looks and sounds like. Ideally they might even ensure that a few such examples are always around while work is in progress. Failing this luxury they would at the very least make sure that there were some excellent pictures and diagrams available as a guide.

Before lifting the lid of our 'bonnets' or 'hoods', we too need to have a clear picture in our minds of the kind of person we would eventually like to be. Very often when people with low self esteem start doing personal development work they find they are clinging to unrealistic objectives for themselves. Perhaps the three most common mistakes are:

1. wanting to turn the clock back and become the person they used to be
2. trying to become a carbon copy of someone whom they

101

admire
3. aiming to be the kind of person whom others would like them to be.

None of the above is intrinsically a 'bad' idea, and each can sometimes prove to be a useful motivational force. But if we are going to use such objectives for inspiration we must make sure that they are both *realistic* and that they *truly fit with our own needs and values*. For example, sometimes keeping handy a photo of ourselves 'in better days' can be an encouragement, but it can also be depressing if the chances of turning the clock back are quite remote. Similarly, gazing admiringly at people on pedestals can inspire us to achieve but it can also be quite de-powering if we are unable to identify with any of our hero's or heroine's strengths. Finally, using other people's encouragement to change ourselves can only be supportive *if* they share our dream and genuinely want us to develop into the kind of person we would like to be.

So I have designed this next exercise to help you bring alive *your ideal image of you*, which although perhaps challenging and inspiring will also be highly achievable.

◇ Exercise – Future Auction

Imagine that in one or two years' time you are going to put *yourself* up for sale in the kind of exclusive auction similar to those used to sell only the very best veteran models! You have been asked to submit a brief description and picture to be included in the glossy brochure.

(Don't forget that once you have become your 'dream model' you will be confident enough to assert your right to decide that you are too valuable to trade in after all!)

While bearing in mind that there are advertising standards to respect, but not forgetting that this will be a much *improved* version of the current 'you', fill in the blanks below. Note that there is also a space for an imaginary photo.

(your name)
....

Most outstanding personal qualities:

1.
....

2.
....

3.
....

Particularly well-skilled at

....

....

Proof of ability to rise to daunting challenges (i.e. during the last year he/she has managed to)

....

....

You can have complete confidence in him/her because

....

....

If you ever have the misfortune to say good-bye to . . . . . . you will always remember him/her because

....

....

In the box below imagine that you are going to submit a photo of the 'new you' set in a typical scenario of your life. Don't forget that once your self esteem has been built up to a consistently high level, many aspects of your lifestyle and relationships are likely to change. So before writing ask yourself:

In one or two years' time:

- What activity would I like most to see myself doing?
- Would I want anyone else with me? (You could include an imaginary new person.)
- How would I like to look? (e.g. clothes, hair, non-verbal expressions etc.)

Beneath the photo, jot down a few descriptive notes – or alternatively let the artist in you do some imaginative sketching.

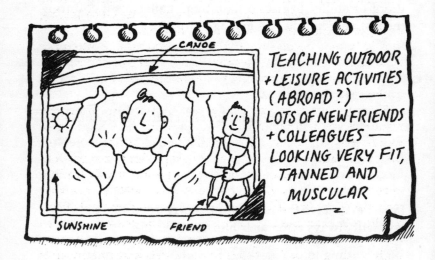

Step 2: **Prepare the Estimate**

In our consumerist culture, reconditioning is rarely a cheap process, its costs being generally high in both time and resources. In the real world (however morally unpalatable this stark economic truth may be), it is often cheaper to opt for a new replacement. Cars are therefore regularly doomed to the scrap yard well before their true sell-by-date, just as employees are often mercilessly replaced long before they have reached their full working potential.

Fortunately, you have made a promise not even to consider the option of 'writing yourself off'! But one implication of this decision is that you may have to 'spend' quite a bit on yourself for a while in order to meet the costs of reconditioning your self esteem. After all, in the business of reconditioning unique veterans only a naïve fool would expect excellent results from a cheap quick-fix! Similarly, in order to make lasting changes in our personality and behaviour we may temporarily have to become relatively big spenders. The difference between us and the loving car owner is that by and large we will be dipping into different kinds of funds to gain access to the currency we need.

Because this is essentially a self-help programme, the resources you will require for this reconditioning programme will largely consist of TIME and ENERGY rather than hard cash or an additional mortgage. Perhaps this is not particularly welcome news for those of you who are already leading very full and busy lives, because I am well aware that sometimes the first two resources can be much more difficult to allocate than money. This is one of the reasons why so many people with low self esteem are becoming increasingly willing to pay fortunes to therapists and pharmacists who promise instant relief for symptoms, and why expensive products such as designer clothes, new cars and luxury holidays are often marketed as having instant morale-and status-boosting qualities. (And of course, in our money-orientated society often the more expensive the 'treat' or 'status symbol', the more tempting it can be to a person with low self esteem.)

If you are among the many who have already spent a small fortune on these kinds of 'emergency boosts' for your self-worth, you might like to try this next exercise – which could prove in the long run to be a much more cost-effective approach.

◊ Exercise – The Estimate

1. How much time per month can I reasonably allocate to completing the exercises in this book and working on some of the root causes of my low self esteem? (4 – 6 hours per month is the minimum usually required to show progress within a few a months.)
   1/2/3/4/5/6/7/8 or ..... hours
2. How much time can I set aside each day to reflect on my progress?
   5 min/10 min/15 min or ..... minutes
3. How much money am I willing, and able, to spend on buying additional resources (e.g. books/courses/tapes/paper/art materials/rewards, etc.)?

   ....
4. What activity or activities would I be willing to sacrifice over the next two months, should I need to make extra time available for reconditioning my self esteem?

   ....
5. What cut-backs on my regular expenditure do I need to make in order to have some extra cash available for my personal development work?

   ....
6. What am I prepared to do in order to increase my energy levels to meet any extra demands on my body, mind and emotions? (e.g. early nights; vitamin supplements; saying 'no' to overtime, etc.)

   ....

Step 3: Complete a Diagnostic Analysis

Now it's strip-down time! Your next task is to scrutinize yourself in order to analyse exactly which factors may be causing you concern about your self esteem and which may be having a positive effect. This information will help you to make much more effective use of the resources you have allocated to your reconditioning programme. You will also have a much clearer idea of which aspects *you*, as a unique individual, may need to replace, improve or simply strengthen in order to become the kind of person you can hold in high esteem.

◊ Exercise – Analysing My Own Strengths and Weaknesses

1. Think of *three* occasions in the last six months when you have felt that you were 'running well' and your self esteem was at a particularly high level. Bring the memories of each occasion back to life either by talking or thinking about them for a while. Re-create an image in your mind of how you looked and sounded. Think about how you were spending most of your time, and with whom you were enjoying contact. Make a few notes and keep these handy so you can use them to prompt your thinking when completing relevant exercises in the following sections.
2. Think of three examples of when your self esteem was rocky and you were 'running sluggishly' or may even have 'crashed'. As above, consider these carefully and make notes to refer to later.
3. Using your notes to start you thinking, complete the following relevant sentences:

'I tend to feel OK about myself when I am:
- being the kind of person who is...'
- using my capacity to feel...'
- using my mind to...'
- using my body to...'
- using my skills to...'
- using my knowledge of...'
- being the kind of friend who...'
- being the kind of relative who...'
- being the kind of employee who...'
- living according to values which respect...'
- perceived by others as being...'
- in the habit of...'

4. Repeat the exercise above, this time starting each sentence this way:
    'I tend *not* to feel OK about myself when I am...'

Step 4: Reinforce the Strong Parts

Very often when our self esteem is at a low ebb an analysis will reveal that we have not been using our strengths to their full capacity – perhaps they may have become rusted or even been forgotten in our 'obsession' with our weaknesses and difficulties. The following exercise will help you to 'polish up' these valuable parts of yourself.

◇ Exercise – Strengthening My Strengths

1. Compose six affirmations for yourself of six important personal strengths or skills which you feel would boost

your self esteem by (see pages 70-72), such as:
- *I am resourceful.*
- *I am loving.*
- *I am an excellent communicator.*

Write these on a postcard and keep them in your bag or diary. Repeat each at least three times a day for *the next week*.

2. On the first day each of the *next three weeks*, select two of these strengths to focus on. Set yourself some specific goals in relation to these strengths, such as:
    - 'I am going to strengthen my capacity for being supportive by giving more compliments to colleagues this week.'
    - 'I am going to stimulate my creativity by finding the time to have a brainstorm before I make decisions or write reports.'
    - 'I am going to strengthen my courage by ringing _____ and making a complaint about...'

3. Remind yourself of your resolution by writing a note in your diary or pinning it up in a prominent place.

Step 5: Clear the Blockages

Unless you have spent a particularly sheltered time cruising along in the quiet lane of life, you will be looking worse for wear inside as well as outside. In Chapter 3 we looked at the way in which unhealed emotional wounds can block the growth and maintenance of healthy self esteem. If you are a relatively elderly model and your emotional health has not been well looked after, this part of the reconditioning process might require a few months' work. But *do not* be tempted to rush through the process. It would be a pointless waste of energy to have reached this stage and then close your bonnet in despair again. Be assured that a relatively short amount of time spent now in unblocking the feeling part of yourself will give you enough positive energy to speed down the motorways of life for as long as your bodywork can stand the pressure!

◇ Exercise – Healing the Inner Hurt

1. For this exercise you might like to use a large sheet of paper, or tape together separate smaller sheets. First, divide your paper as in the Table below, so that you have a column for each five-year period of your life thus far. Then use this 'chart' to note down any significant emotional wounds you can remember experiencing. (Obviously the longer you have lived, the more emotional wounds you may have experienced and therefore the more paper you will need!)

   Remember that when selecting which wounds to note down, always use your own feelings and values as a guide. What can feel like a hurt or disappointment to one person can sometimes seem like a non-event to hundreds of others. Also take into consideration your age and circumstances at the time, as these will obviously have affected the degree of emotional damage. Finally, don't forget that – in respect of the healing process – probably the most significant aspect of all will be the way the hurt was handled.

2. If you feel that your memory of Chapter 3 needs a little jogging, take a break from this exercise and re-read it.

   If, on the other hand, you remember the step-by-step process which I have described, write down beside each of the wounds you have listed which stage of healing you have reached with each one.

3. Review your analysis and mark with a star or coloured pen the 'wounds' that you think still need some attention because they are blocking you emotionally from either:
   – being able to feel good about yourself or the rest of the world

or
- being as successful in your personal or professional life as you would like to be.

4. Note down some goals. The following are some examples of action you could use for different kinds of wounds at different stages in their healing process:
   - *Talk to my sister about my jealousy (Essential stage 5 – PERSPECTIVE).*
   - *Send away for an Adult Education prospectus (Essential stage 4 – COMPENSATION).*
   - *Stop pretending that I am not disappointed about losing that job (Essential stage 2 – EXPRESSION).*
   - *Ask Jo if I can go and stay for a weekend (Essential stage 3 – COMFORT).*
   - *Set-up a self-help group (Bonus stage 6 – CHANNELLING)*

5. Add a review date beside each goal and mark it in your diary now!

Step 6: Strengthen the Weak Areas

No doubt you also have some parts which will always be rather inferior to other parts (perhaps the genes that came off the Friday afternoon production line!). Many of these you will have to accept and live with, but now that you are examining yourself it is important to check that these weak areas are not in the driving seat of your life. You can assert more control over them if you:

- Make sure that they are as strong as their potential will allow them to be.
- Take care not to let them take too much stress and strain, and see that they are well supported by the stronger parts.
- Keep checking for deterioration and contamination.

In my experience, people with low self esteem tend to do quite the *opposite*. Very often they are in the habit of unconsciously allowing their weaknesses to become a much more dominant force in their lives than they need be. Here are some common mistakes which I am sure you will instantly recognize:

Unnecessarily Highlighting Weak Areas to Others

- 'You can't miss me, I am the skinny one with the raucous laugh and the buck teeth.'
- 'I pity you having to share an office with me, I'm the untidiest person born this century.'
- 'I hope you'll all manage to stay awake to the end of this presentation – I know I do have a tendency to belabour my points.'
- 'I know I shouldn't be eating this, I'm spotty enough already.'

Expending Crippling Amounts of Energy (and Money) on Eradicating a Weakness

- trying every new diet or cure that comes onto the market
- spending so much time in the gym or beauty parlour that there is little left for enjoyment and relaxation
- hanging on stubbornly to unsuitable tasks and jobs which could be delegated to others who could do them much more efficiently.

Alienating Others by Boring Them with Regrets and Wishful Thinking

- 'If only I was a little taller/not so hairy/younger/less tone-deaf', etc.
- 'I wish I were like you, you're organized/so creative', etc.

- 'If only I had the persistence to study, or practise more, when I was younger.'

In contrast, another 'method of coping' with weaknesses which people with low self esteem use is that of trying to **deny its existence either to themselves or others**. This often means that they frequently waste their own and other people's energy.

For example, someone who:

- has very little aptitude for mental arithmetic insisting he can manage without a calculator
- has virtually nil sense of direction but refuses to ask the way or consult the map
- spends hours trying to think up a new excuse for not going to another big party or conference which she 'knows' she will not enjoy or be able to shine at
- repairs zips on jeans which have had too much flesh crammed inside them, rather than just buying a new pair in a larger size.

Finally, people with low self esteem sometimes adopt a style of denial which involves **'projecting' their weakness on to other people**. This results in, for example:

- nagging others to correct a fault which they have not accepted or learned to control in themselves
- becoming a martyr to the cause of helping others sort their problems out while not paying attention to the mess in their own department (or life!).

◇ Exercise – Reinforcing My Weaknesses

1. Re-read the above section and note down any bad habits which you may have developed in relation to your weaknesses.

2. List your main weaknesses under the following headings:
   - Body
   - Mind and intellect
   - General personality
   - Behaviour in relation to care and development of self
   - Behaviour in relation to others

3. Taking three different coloured pens, mark the ones which:
   a) you cannot change
   b) you could change, but which are not worth expending energy on because you can live with them
   c) you want to change and are (or will be!) actively working on.
   d) For each of the weaknesses that fall under (a) or (b), write a sentence which assertively acknowledges them but *either* highlights a compensatory feature (perhaps taken from your list of strengths?), such as:
      - 'I accept that I am untidy but I take responsibility for the consequences of my mess.'
      - 'I accept that my nose is long but I have big eyes.'
      - 'I accept that I am not a natural leader but I have the courage to ask for help and advice when I am struggling.'

   or acknowledges the positive (or potentially positive aspects) of your weakness when it is fully under your control, such as:
      - 'Under my control, my shyness helps me to be a good listener and be a more objective observer.'
      - 'Under my control, my bossiness can help me become a charismatic leader.'
      - 'Under my control, my greediness helps to motivate me.'
      - 'Under my control, my aggression helps me to protect my own and others' rights.'
      - 'Under my control, my meanness can help me to avoid being abused by people who want my money.'

   e) Read this list out loud to yourself several times over the next few days, using a strong assertive voice. For even stronger reinforcement, read it out loud to a

114

supportive friend or group.

f) Later (after you have worked on [a] and [b]), note
down some specific action which you are taking (or will
take!) to improve the weaknesses listed under (c). For
example:

- 'I am not assertive enough, so I have booked a
  place on an Assertiveness Training course starting
  in October.'
- 'I am not as fit as I was in my twenties, so I will
  walk up the stairs at work each day and join the
  gym.'
- 'I have a natural tendency to be disorganized, so I
  am borrowing a book from the library on Time
  Management and will set aside some money for a
  new filing system/software/extra secretarial help,
  etc.'
- 'When I am over-anxious I become too controlling,
  so I will ask my colleagues to tell me when this
  starts to happen and then I will take steps to
  reduce my stress or control my anxiety.'
- 'I am not a good driver, so I will let others drive
  me or take trains.'
- 'My mind is sluggish and has never been used to
  its full potential, so I am enrolling on an
  educational programme in the Autumn.'

Step 7: Replace the Old
and Out-dated

Although we are essentially in the business of renovation, it
would be crazy not to leave yourself the option of replacing
some of your parts with more up-to-date versions – especially
if, by so doing, you know you are likely to run with far fewer
troubles.

The parts that most people with low self esteem benefit from replacing are:

1. *General negative beliefs* embedded in our subconscious – these include 'messages' about ourselves, the world and other people which, whether we like it or not, may have a considerable impact on the way we run our lives (such as 'Life is hard;' 'Other people always let you down;' 'Marriage is a necessary evil;' 'Love never lasts;' 'Power corrupts')

2. *Long-established self-destructive behaviourial habits* (such as setting unrealistic goals; being late for everything; letting others speak first; breaking off relationships as soon as they become comfortable; playing too safe; being over-protective, etc.)

Very often these are parts of us which feel *integral to our personality* and we often view them as either *normal* or *irrefutably true*. This is usually because we started to acquire them in early childhood when our personalities were still forming, or because they are continually reinforced in our subconscious minds. Nowadays we are likely to have a hotchpotch of 'mind messages' and habits which we have picked up not just from traditional early role-models such as our parents, teachers and religious leaders, but also from other powerful subconscious influences such as the mass media and advertising. Because we have no recollection of having acquired these aspects of ourselves (and often cannot remember ourselves without them), initially it is quite difficult to view them as *learned additions* to the core of 'us'. *But* learn them we most certainly did – and therefore, *unlearn* them we most certainly can!

The first step must be to identify these parts and bring them fully into our conscious awareness so that we can then take appropriate action to make sure that they are replaced. I am well aware that this personal development exercise is much easier to talk about than do, so watch out for excuses and denial. Take heart from the memory of some of the other worthwhile changes you have effected in your life (such as a move to a better office or the acquisition of a new car or even company). At the outset these endeavours most likely required several tedious and sometimes heart-wrenching trips to the scrap yard or rubbish bin. But I am sure you also remember how quickly the pain of parting with this 'rubbish' vanished once the transition had been completed!

◇ Exercise – Replacing the Obsolete Parts of Me

1. Write one of each of the following incomplete sentences at the top of some cards (large index ones would be ideal).
    a) 'Although I know it's OK to........, I still feel guilty when........'
    b) 'Although I know I do not need to........, I still feel obligated to........'

c) 'I wish I could stop thinking.................'
d) 'I wish I could stop acting like.............'
e) 'I wish I could stop feeling so.............'
f) 'I know it's silly of me but I always/never...........'
g) 'I'd like to get rid of my prejudices about...........'

2. Carry these cards around with you for a couple of weeks and use them to note down your annoying obsolete beliefs and habits.
3. Using the strategies in Section Two for reference, note down the following:

    a) *HOW* your subconscious acquired its sabotaging 'mind message' or you learned your behaviourial habit (remember this search for insight is not about passing the buck, it's about helping you to reinforce your belief that you can change).

    b) *ACTION* you are going to take in order to replace each with *your* choice of belief, attitude or behaviour. You may find it helpful to re-read appropriate chapters of Section Two before deciding on what action to take (e.g. assertiveness or stress management).

Example A

'I wish I had the nerve to complain about the............... like Tony does.'

HOW: 'Mind messages' originating from 1) Mum (who always said it wasn't worth the fuss), 2) school (where teachers were always right), 3) working-class culture (fed 'victim' in me)

ACTION: Talk to Tony for support and practise writing and reading some assertive scripts (pages 85-8)

Example B

'If only I weren't so untidy.......'

HOW: Bad habit left over from student days
ACTION: Go to battle with the habit (see Chapter 4)

Step 8: Check the Connections

Now that you have checked each individual part and have acquired some new ones, it is time to start thinking about how everything fits together. After all, however sound and strong each individual part of us is, we cannot use our full power and potential if our 'whole' is not functioning as a harmonious unit. I have often found that people with low self esteem feel 'disconnected' inside. In fact they frequently admit to the fear that they may be 'schizophrenic' because they experience themselves as a number of completely different people working in isolation. Sometimes they can relate these 'people' to different roles they play in life, or ' moods' brought on by variations in their health, the weather or even the position of the moon. Such feelings are not a sign of 'madness' but they do indicate a degree of inner disharmony which can undoubtedly undermine our sense of confidence.

If you have a tendency to feel internally disjointed, try this next exercise, which is a new self-help version of the kind which I have used for many years to help people to strengthen their sense of identity.

◇ Exercise – Connecting Up the Whole of Me

Although in the earlier exercises in this programme you have done some analysis work on your personality, now is the time to do an in-depth inspection. As you will find that this next exercise can take up a considerable amount of time (at least a good two hours), I suggest that you read it through before planning your 'timetable' for completing it. You could complete it in a series of stages.

1. Do a **brainstorm** of all the different aspects of you. Put your name in the centre of a large sheet of paper and then randomly jot down any words which come into

119

your head when you think about you (such as *thoughtful, shy, bossy, stubborn, gentle, workaholic, perfectionist, scatter-brain, day-dreamer, reader, analyst, organizer, introvert, party-lover*). Don't forget that when you are doing a brainstorm, in order to make full use of the creative side of your brain it is important not to censor ideas even if at the time they may seem silly or contradictory. If you allow yourself to free-associate you will automatically stimulate your creativity and will then be much more likely to produce information that the more logical, analytical side of your brain has forgotten or not noticed. You will be able to edit out the irrelevant words later.

Leave the sheet of paper around for a couple of days, adding words as you 'observe' yourself in action. Also take some quiet time to reflect back on your past life as well, because in so doing you may well be reminded of other aspects of yourself which you had forgotten.

2. Now take *eight* different *large index cards*. Look again at your 'brainstorm paper' and **list** the words that seem to go together on each one (one card, for example, might list

thoughtful, gentle, reader; another *stubborn, bossy, perfectionist*). Leave out the ones which are duplicated or 'silly'. (You may find that you do not need all eight cards, on the other hand try not to use any more than this.)

3. At the top of each card write a **'nick-name'** which you can use to describe these particular aspects of yourself (e.g. 'The Clown', 'The Achiever', 'Battleaxe', etc.)

    Beside each name add a small symbol to act as a memory aid (see example below.)

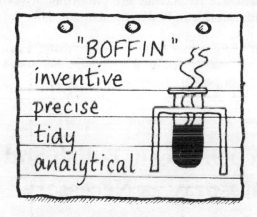

4. Imagine that these different parts of you are a **team** who have been given a task to accomplish together, and that you have been chosen as their leader because you are renowned for being able to help even the most disparate of groups interact usefully together.
5. Choose an imaginary **task** (or two!) for the team to complete. This could be relevant to your life, but it might be more enlightening and useful to use one with which you are not so familiar (such as erecting a marquee, fundraising for the rain forests, opening a new shop, etc.)
6. Using your cards to help you, **plan** how you are going to get this diverse group working most effectively together. Remembering that closed 'cliques' are to be discouraged, look for natural pairings and potential conflicts and note

how you would use and handle these. Also look at how you can help each individual 'person' feel part of the group by using his or her particular skills or aptitudes.

7. Use Creative Visualization (see pages 93-4) to imagine yourself briefing the group and then observing them competently completing their task.

8. Now imagine that, since your project was so successful, your team is now looking for other work to do together. Jot down some ideas on tasks they could accomplish and then write out a concise advert or design a leaflet which you could use to market the potential of your well-managed, interestingly diverse team.

Finally, don't forget that this incredible team is always on hand, free of charge for you – so you need never feel overwhelmed or powerless again!

Step 9: Clean, Polish and Respray as Necessary

Once the inner you has been sorted and strengthened, it is time to take a look at your bodywork! Maybe some of you already have a gleaming showroom sheen and will need only a light dusting, while others may feel so different internally that only a complete 'respray' will do them justice. I would guess that the majority of readers will just need to touch up their scratches and rusty patches and embellish themselves with a luxurious wax and shine.

People with low self esteem often believe that an important criteria of self-worth is a person's ability to live life without caring about how he or she looks. I think this is a wishful myth. Although I can fully appreciate the *feeling* behind not wanting to care about image and external appearance, I think it is important to remember that the attraction of this myth is usually rooted either in a lack of unconditional love or frustration at being too dependent on pleasing others.

In the real world the truth is that people (and even most animals!) with high self esteem do care very considerably about their external appearance and try to ensure that it is, at the very least, always 'good-enough'. They will, of course, vary considerably in the amount of time, money and energy they spend on improving and maintaining their outer image. After all, some may actually enjoy the 'art' of looking good and therefore give it high priority, while others may prefer to take a more business-like approach. Also, some may choose to look like a model from *Vogue*, while others may opt for comfort over the latest fashion. But the common denominators seem to be that people with good self esteem:

- are never afraid, embarrassed, or too busy to take regular long hard looks in mirrors and appraise the image they see
- enjoy looking good and cherish genuine compliments and constructive criticism about their appearance
- ensure that their clothes, hair and accessories accentuate their strengths, minimize their weaknesses, harmonize with their personality and do not up-stage their skills
- are willing and able to adapt their image to get what *they* want and need, and keep pace with their own personal development
- can happily seek advice and opinions from others, but ultimately make their own decisions and take responsibility for being judge and jury of their overall image
- put comfort high on their priority list, so that once their clothes, hair and other accessories have been selected they can relax and forget them and get on with whatever else they want or need to do
- do not choose to adopt an image which others find over-powering or which consistently jars with the environment they choose to be in
- do not spend more money, time or energy on their

external image than they can realistically afford
– are prepared to fight for their right to look good and feel comfortable should people with more power make unreasonable demands (e.g. unnecessary commands to wear unflattering, stiff uniforms).

◇ Exercise – Improving My External Image

1. Read the above list of characteristics and mark those which you are still *honestly* unable to note in your own feelings, behaviour and appearance.
2. Note down what you are going to do about each area in which you are still having difficulty. For example:

– Start enjoying and accepting compliments (saying thank you instead of 'Well, I like your...;' or 'It's only a...').
– Get up 15 minutes earlier each day so you have time to look after your appearance.
– Start keeping a file of magazine cuttings which show the image you would like to have.
– Make an appointment with an image consultant.
– Go on a diet and/or join a gym.
– Go to the Charity Shop with the clothes which are now too tight/big/inappropriate/wrong colour, etc.
– Leave your credit cards at home when you go in to town to help limit impulse buying.
– Work out a budget for clothes and learn and practise the Broken Record technique (pages 77-9) to help you resist overbearing salespeople.
– Use Fogging (pages 79-81) to stop the put-downs from others.
– Use Negative Enquiry (pages 83-5) to get feedback from..........

Step 10: Lubricate and Fill with Fuel

Once everything is back in place and strongly connected, we need to 'oil' ourselves thoroughly and fill our tanks with good quality 'fuel'.

The mixture of *oil* which I would strongly recommend to keep the wheels of self esteem running smoothly is a combination of the following ingredients:

1. *consistent loving self-care*
2. *dependable supportive nurturing from others*
3. *good-quality fun and humour*
4. *periods of recuperative rest and relaxation.*

The *fuel* needed to fire our self esteem into successful action is a mixture including these kinds of ingredients:

1. *a high-quality, nourishing diet free of harmful toxins*
2. *oxygen derived from exercise and fresh air*
3. *stimulating intellectual and creative input*
4. *positive affirmations*
5. *motivational and encouraging feedback from others.*

Do you fuel yourself with enough of the above? If you have only shaky self esteem, I doubt it. It is much more likely that you have spent a lifetime hill-climbing and rally-driving on two-star! You have probably been programmed to think that the ingredients listed above are luxuries or selfish extravagances which you can ill afford or do not deserve.

When we are still young and sturdy, we can survive reasonably well on low-grade fuel and we can even allow ourselves to run dry occasionally. But once we have reached veteran status (but still want access to the fast lane), we must make sure that we are constantly replenishing ourselves with premium grade! If we do not we will most certainly burn ourselves out prematurely or seize up with a massive loss of confidence. So use the next exercise to help you break some of the self-destructive habits which may be influencing the quality of 'fuel' with which you are feeding yourself and your self esteem. But before starting, be warned that *you will need access to your diary!*

◇ Exercise – Fuel for the Fast Lane

1. Take your diary and with a brightly coloured pen strike through at least one whole day (or two half-days, if you must!) and *immediately* write in 'Self-care Day'. This may be during the weekend, the working week or even a holiday, but it MUST be *within the next month. Take this first step NOW, before reading on.*
2. Did you do it? If you did, well done! You can now move on to Step 11 without completing the rest of this exercise.

    If you didn't (and I think you are likely to be in the company of the majority!), we are now going to identify some reasons why you didn't.

    Being scrupulously honest with yourself, note any resistance you put up to my suggestion (in other words, your excuse!). Did you perhaps say something to yourself such   as:
    'I can't (or won't) because:
    – every minute is accounted for'
    – I can't let others down'
    – I can't afford it – I need the money'
    – I don't need it'
    – this month is just a bad month – in a couple of months' time...'
    – someone might see it and think...'
    – I won't be told how to run my life'
    – I spend too much time as it is on...'
    – I can't find my diary'
    – I don't keep a diary.'
3. Ask yourself if this is a *common reaction* for you? Do you often hear yourself making these or any of the other

'excuses' when faced with the challenge of planning your own self-care? If you have answered 'yes' then you are probably stuck in a self-destructive habit of belief or behaviour. Re-read Chapter 4 and plan (and take!) your action!

4. While the Strategy for Breaking Self-destructive Habits is fresh in your mind, make a note of any other bad habits you may have hanging around in your mind or personality which also need work. Give at least three an 'Action Day' and mark them in your diary.

HABIT	*ACTION DAY*
late nights	next Monday
over use of the car	
too much pre-packaged food	
smoking	January 1st
skipping lunches	tomorrow
over-stressful leisure activities	
or holidays	
being too tired for fun	

Step 11: Check for Safety

However brilliant and powerful you may now look and feel, it would be pointless to leave the showroom without casting a very careful eye over your ability to cope with the inevitable hazards you will meet in the traffic of the real world. In your childhood, safety may not have been a priority issue. The preparation many of us had when we were young for even the everyday threats we encounter today is likely to have been inadequate. But just as seat-belts, airbags and side-impact bars have been invented to protect the modern driver from tyrants of the road and other potential perils, so in the psychological world we have been developing self-protective strategies and techniques to help the vulnerable defend themselves against life's bullies and injustice. The ones which I have found most invaluable I have already described in chapters 3, 4 and 5. Now it's crunch time! We are going to test your understanding of these important strategies and also your ability to translate them into useful tools which you will use to protect yourself and your self esteem.

◇ Exercise – Testing My Self-protective Strategies

1. Skim through the headings of Chapter 5 and re-read the sections which you may need to revise.
2. Rewrite the following, using language that will help you to defend yourself from your own negative thinking when you are going through rough terrain (use GEE strategy – pages 68-9 – and Reframing – pages 69-70 – to help you).
   'I've had such an awful day; everything has gone wrong that could possibly have gone wrong. I don't know what's happening. I seem to be going backwards – I can't cope anymore. Anyway I'm not sure what the point of it all is. After all, in a rat race only rats can win – if you can't beat them you might as well join them...no, I don't want your sympathy...in fact don't come near me, I'm bad news.'
3. Think of an unpleasant encounter you have been putting off dealing with for a while, such as:
   - a phone call to a relative you know is likely to try to make you feel guilty about not visiting very often
   - a friend whom you do not want to go on holiday with anymore
   - an angry, abusive customer whose complaint you have investigated and decided is unjustified
   - a well-meaning but inefficient colleague who has been letting you or the company down
   - a neighbour who has started to cut his or her lawn at 8 o'clock every Sunday morning

– your touchy teenage son or daughter whom you suspect may be 'up to something' but you are not sure what.

4. Now prepare yourself by doing the following:

    a) Write your opening Script (pages 85-9).

    b) Write down your response to any negative reaction or criticism you are likely to receive (you could use Broken Record, Fogging or Negative Assertion – pages 77-9, 79-81 or 81-3).

    c) If appropriate, compose a phrase which you could use to bring out a criticism or negative feeling which you suspect is lurking 'under the carpet' (use Negative Enquiry, pages 83-5).

    d) Note which Anchor you are going to use to keep you positive (Anchoring, pages 72-3).

    e) Note what you are going to do to become calm and positive before you meet or ring them (you could use Affirmations and one of the Quick-Fix Relaxers on pages 70-72 or 91).

    f) Note how you are going to get support for yourself both before and after the encounter.

    g) Note how you are going to reward yourself (whether you succeeded or just courageously tried).

Step 12: Test-drive for Performance and Ecology

Reconditioned people as well as cars need a gentle 'trial period' prior to hitting the headlines with the success of their super-confidence! Only when we have tested 'this year's model' out on our own particular road can we see what adjustments we may need to make. Once we are in action and can feel, and observe, the *consequences of our new attitudes and behaviour*, we can begin to fine-tune ourselves.

When you have been taking a back seat in life for too many years, it is frustrating to be told to 'drive slowly' and 'keep to the quiet lanes'. Your understandable urge is to put your foot down and make up for all that lost time. But if you do, not only will you run the risk of premature burnout and a crash, you will miss out on the joy and satisfaction that can be gained from knowing that you are also able to function in a way that *uses your potential to its best advantage while at the same time being mindful and respectful of the environment in which you are 'driving'.*

Ecology is as important an issue in personal development as it is in driving. Just as reconditioning can increase the potential power of a car, self esteem building undoubtedly boosts personal power. In my view it is essential that power of any description should be used, not just in the interests of those who have it, but also (whenever possible) in *the interests of those who cannot have the same advantage*. As I travel around in my role as a spokesperson for personal development work,

I frequently meet confrontational journalists who quite rightly challenge the ethics of what I am doing. The kind of questions I am most commonly asked are:

> *'Aren't you creating a self-satisfied élite who will use your techniques and strategies to feather their own nests without caring about the masses in the world who can never be as confident and successful as they are?'*

or

> *'Aren't you creating another kind of "junkie" – whose sole interest is in how to get their next "shot" of therapy and who will not even notice the pain and suffering of others or the destruction of the planet on which they are living?'*

My experience of what actually happens when a person's self esteem has been boosted is, in fact, quite the reverse. In the last few years I have begun to run more and more advanced personal development courses and it has been interesting to note how outward-looking the people on these courses have become. Having achieved an acceptable level of confidence for themselves and found some stable happiness in their own lives, their thoughts seem to turn quite spontaneously towards helping others. Indeed, an eavesdropper on these courses would very likely more often hear constructive discussions on community and world issues than the tears and angst of personal pain.

It is low, not high self esteem that fuels selfish and egocentric attitudes and behaviour. How many bullying road-hogs *or* crawlers in the slow lane do you find stopping at the scene of an accident or breakdown? The first may not even notice because their attention is focused on boosting their self-worth by going faster than anyone else. The second are frequently too frightened of rejection or of 'doing the wrong thing' to interfere. Indeed, if I were the person in need, I would be grateful that neither of these types of people had stopped. If they had (perhaps in order to impress), it is likely that I would have had to expend energy keeping myself from feeling either *inferior* (the road-hog would no doubt have had to let me know that this never happens to him or her) or *irritated* (because the crawler might be dithering about the best thing to be seen to be doing). When I require help, I know that I prefer to receive it from someone who is emotionally strong enough to be able to temporarily set aside his or her own self esteem needs.

Understandably, as our self esteem grows we also seem to find ourselves becoming particularly attracted towards helping others build up their own self-worth. In Section Four we will be looking at ways in which we can use our increased personal power to boost others' self esteem. But for the moment we are still checking that our own house is in sound ethical order so that we can rest assured that we will be *routinely* operating in a way which *we* can be proud of.

> *Self-respect is a fundamental key to self esteem. We cannot hope to feel consistently good about ourselves unless we are also consistently living a life which respects our own values.*

The following exercise is designed to help you clarify your own everyday 'rules of the road' so that you have some concisely defined criteria according to which you can more easily judge whether you are indeed a person worth respecting.

◊ Exercise – My Own 'Highway Code'

1. Over a period of a week or so, complete the following sentences as many times as you can (but keep your analyst's hat firmly locked away for the moment!).

✔ I have a right to use my personal power to (for example):
  – *ask for what I want*
  – *be happy*
  – *protect my reputation*
  – *defend those I love*

– *better my health.*

✔ When using my personal power in relation to others, I should always (for example):
– *think first*
– *respect the weak*
– *assess whether or not I need the other person*
– *be honest.*

✔ I should let other people take responsibility for their:
– *feelings*
– *own happiness*
– *ethics.*

✔ I aim to be the kind of person who never uses personal power:
– *to deliberately hurt others*
– *to damage the environment*
– *to make others look small*
– *without thinking of the consequences.*

✔ I would like to use my personal power to help:
– *make the world a safer place*
– *others stand up for their rights*
– *manage the department more efficiently.*

Now read your lists with a critical eye and scribble your comments. Underline or highlight the words which have the most significance for you.

In relation to using the increased personal power your self esteem will bring you, list the SIX most important 'rules of the road' for you. For example:

– *be happy*
– *think before acting*
– *be honest*
– *let other people take responsibility for their own ethics*
– *do not intentionally hurt others*

– make the world a safer place.

Enjoy the Drive!
(Don't forget that using your self esteem should also be exciting, rewarding and fun!)

7

Regular Maintenance

Brand new cars (so I am told!) rarely need attention in their first few years of life. Unless you have been jinxed with a faulty model or have subjected it to extreme adverse conditions, all you are supposed to need to do is keep them topped up with good-quality petrol, wash off the grime and make sure they are regularly serviced.

A vintage car is, of course, another matter. To keep one of these special vehicles in prime condition you need to be willing, and able, to offer vigilant care. Such cars should never be owned by the reckless or lazy. But to their devoted fans, the extra time, energy and consideration they demand is rarely begrudged.

Just yesterday, my daughter's 18-year-old boyfriend James bought (with his own hard-earned money!) a stunning 1967 white sports car. To James, this car's obvious need for care and attention is part of its charm. When, for example, he noticed the brakes needed adjusting, his response was: 'I don't mind, I shall *enjoy* doing it.' Although I am aware that he would be unlikely to say 'no' should a fairy godmother appear one day with the latest and brightest model, it is great to see him currently beaming with excitement at the thought not just of driving, but also of maintaining his beautiful veteran.

I hope by the end of this chapter you will be just as excited about the challenge of maintaining your renovated self esteem in equally pristine condition!

Seriously, though, I do think these 'maintenance projects' are comparable. Those of us who have had to put our self-image through a major reconditioning process will also always have to keep a careful eye on its progress. And just as James had a choice between taking a negative or a positive view about his task, there are also two ways we can approach the job of providing ongoing care for our self esteem. We can feel resentful about having to 'work at it' and ache with justifiable jealousy of those who take their confidence for granted. Or we can choose to *enjoy* our necessary caretaking duties. So, although this kind of personal development work is not as exciting as the 'renovation' kind, if we approach it positively we will be much more likely to find the fun and many excuses for pampering within it!

In this book we have often focused on the destructive effects of bad habits; now it's time to turn our attention to the potential positive effects of some good ones. The key to any good maintenance programme is *routine*. First we must establish an easy, non-time-consuming way of regularly *checking the 'temperature' of our self esteem*. Secondly, we have to plan time for making a more specific and detailed check on the way we are 'running' to ensure that we have not slipped back into any bad habits which may be surreptitiously undermining all the good work we have done on ourselves.

In the last couple of years I have started to develop programmes of psychological exercises which are designed to be used regularly, like physical workouts. Many of these I have produced in the form of cassettes which, because they are so 'user friendly', have proved to be an exceedingly successful way to establish good maintenance habits. Very often people use them while they are engaged in other routines such as travelling to and from work or doing household chores. Doing this not only saves time but can transform a mundane and already established routine into a constructive self-nurturing experience!

So why not try this 'user-friendly' method to help you with this part of the programme? You can use the cassette I have made to accompany this book or you can substitute or supplement it with a *home-made recording* of your own. You can do this by selecting and adapting the questions in the following exercise to suit your particular needs and circumstances. (Don't forget to leave long enough gaps for you to answer or reflect, to save you the bother of continually turning the tape on and off.)

Alternatively, another way of helping yourself develop a good 'maintenance habit' is to *write or type out a list of the key questions and photocopy a few months' supply*. You can then clip these checklists into your diary at appropriate intervals.

Finally, for the computer buffs among you, why not programme the questionnaire and reminders into your *personal organizers*, or even (if you are very brilliant) install a tailor-made piece of software!

But let's come down to earth again, because all you need for the moment is a humble pencil and a few of sheets of paper. Before devising your own clever methods, try doing my checklist below. I have designed this one to be used once a week. You can of course continue to use it (if you find my car metaphor helpful) or just treat it as a base from which to create one of your own.

◇ Exercise – Maintaining My Self Esteem

1. Work through the checklist below and tote up your final score. (Note that I have included references to appropriate sections in the book, if you should need to do a little revision as you go along!)
2. Make a note of what you intend to do more (or less) of during the next week in order to maintain an acceptable level of self esteem.
3. Revise the checklist as required to suit your needs more specifically.

Don't forget to make it quick and easy to use, and to establish a routine for completing it.

SELF ESTEEM MAINTENANCE CHECKLIST

To assess the current state of your self esteem and appraise its everyday care over the past week, you can use the small boxes beside each heading in either of two ways:

1. inserting a simple tick or cross (who hasn't got time to do this?!)
2. scoring yourself 1 – 10 for each box. When these figures are totalled you will then have a percentage figure which could be entered on a graph, giving you a quick reference guide that could be very useful when you are doing your major self esteem 'servicing' at a later date.

The first time you use the checklist it would be advisable to read my explanatory notes after each question before scoring yourself.

❑ 1. Is My Gauge Reading Good-enough?

Mark on the gauge below the current rating of your self esteem today. Taking into consideration the stage you are at in your self esteem building programme and what may be going on in your life at the moment, assess whether or not your reading is 'good-enough'. You could also mark yourself on significant 'events' or activities of the week which may

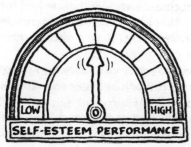

relate to your high and low points.
❏ 2. Has My Temperature Chart Been Stable Enough?

Draw your own recording line on the chart below, according to how you have felt on a daily basis. (A rough assessment is all you need.) If it has been quite unstable, note down the main factors you think may have contributed towards its highs and lows.

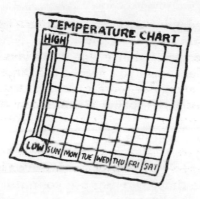

❏ 3. Is My Windscreen Clear Enough?

Can you still see the 'dream you' ahead? How clear and vivid are your long-term goals at the moment? For example, have you been keeping yourself motivated by visualizing your future success (pages 93-4), talking freely with supportive friends about positive outcomes you expect and doing things in the present which keep you emotionally in touch with your destination?

❏ 4. Am I 'Driving' Sensibly?

Have you succeeded in avoiding unrealistic goals which could set you up for failure? Are you sticking to your step-by-step action plans? Have you achieved what you set out to do this week?

Did you plan and organize yourself well enough? Did you,

for example, make good use of all your strengths; manage to keep to time schedules and obtain a good balance between stimulating challenge and peaceful consolidation? Did you keep control of any self-sabotaging tendencies or did you sink back into any old bad habits? Have you been using your full potential? (Chapter 4)

❑ 5. Have I Managed to Keep in the Right Gear?

Have you used your assertive, passive and aggressive behaviour gears appropriately and in ways that have maximized the use of your energy? Did you stand up for yourself or others when you needed to? Did you choose to conserve your energy or protect your interests by taking a back seat occasionally? (pages 73-88)

❑ 6. Have I Been Sparking Consistently?

Have you been able to maintain a positive frame of mind for most of the time? Did you use your affirmations and other strategies to help you chase away any negative demons which may have crept in? (pages 66-75)

❑ 7. Are My Connections Still Sound?

Have you managed to maintain a good link between your heart and your head? Were you able to remain emotionally controlled when you wanted to? Were you aware enough of your feelings and able to use your body's warning signals to help you manage any fear, anxiety or anger you may have felt? (pages 89-97)

❑ 8. Is My Bodywork Still Gleaming?

Have you kept up your 'high self esteem appearance'? Is it obvious to anyone looking at you that you are someone who has self-pride and takes very good care of his or her body? Are you still presenting a confident, positive image of yourself to the world? Does your home and your desk at work reflect an impression that is worthy of you?

❏ 9. Did I Use Garage and Recovery Services When I Needed Them?

Did you fuel yourself up with good-enough food and sleep? Have you arranged enough support for yourself? Were your friends and colleagues able to meet your needs adequately? Did you give yourself enough rest and recuperation?

❏ 10. Have I Been Respectful of My 'Highway Code'?

Have you been living in tune with your values? Have you given enough (and not too much!) thought to the feelings and needs of the people around you this week? Have you also been considerate towards your environment and the wider world as well?

Major Service

However cautiously we may drive our car and however diligent we are in doing its weekly checks, we all know that we'd be foolish and irresponsible not to subject it to a major annual inspection. Similarly, all sorts of nasty deterioration can take place beneath the glossy exteriors of even the most successful among us, if a thorough 'introspection' does not take place at least once a year.

Very often people say that they use their annual holiday to do this kind of deep personal reflection. If you are in the habit of making your holidays work successfully for you like this, you may not need this chapter. But if you are more like me and try to reserve these precious times for 'crashing out', escaping and having some well-earned fun, then you might be interested in this guide to a DIY service routine which can be slotted in quite easily to a quiet weekend. The dutiful people who have completed their weekly maintenance checks might even be able to do it one evening!

Once again I must beg a large slice of writer's licence in the use of my metaphor. I am particularly aware that the service routines of even the most glamorous vintage cars are unlikely to start with a review of their achievements. But because cars miss out on this luxury, why should our self esteem?!

◊ Exercise – My Annual 'Introspection'

1. Work through each section in the checklist below, asking yourself the relevant questions and noting down any specific action you want to take to improve or boost your self esteem during the next year.
2. Choose a maximum of *six* resolutions for yourself for the following year (any more and you would probably be setting yourself up for failure). You may find a clue to what these could be from different themes which may reoccur as you work through the checklist (e.g. time pressures, boredom, family, friends). Make two copies of this list – put one away in your personal development file so that you can use it to check up on your progress at your next self esteem service, and pin the other up on your notice board.

CHECKLIST FOR ANNUAL SELF ESTEEM SERVICE

❑ Review of Achievements

List the experiences which have boosted your self esteem this year. Some of these may be *specific achievements* which are easy to identify, but others may be more general and have more to do with times when you have been particularly *respectful of your own values and your needs for health and happiness*. You may well find it helpful to refer back to your

'Highway Code' (pages 132-4) and the list of goals which you set for yourself last year.

Did you have a reward for each of these achievements? If not, don't forget to include these in your action plan!

Personal
For example:
- getting engaged/married or happily divorced!
- having a son/daughter
- achieving............... at tennis/cricket/golf, etc.
- raising.............. for charity
- becoming chairperson of the local........ party/ organization
- making myself understood in Greece
- my voluntary work with.............
- my support for the successful campaign to............
- achieving more balance in my life
- being healthy.

Action for the future...

Work
For example:
- achieving my target 10 out of 12 months
- being asked to present a report to....................................
- my first trip abroad for the company
- resolving the conflict with...
- getting short-listed for..
- passing............. exams
- the reference which............... gave me
- being much more direct and honest
- being more of a risk-taker in negotiations.

Action for the future:...

❏ General Wear and Tear

List the major knocks and dents your self esteem has received. These may have originated from a wide variety of sources

143

including you, other specific people, an event or the media. Don't forget to look out for any unhealed emotional wounds or 'unfinished business' such as relationship difficulties that need to be sorted out or assertive complaints to be made.

Work/Career
- not getting a promotion
- low summer sales
- racist/sexist jokes from.........
- not having the annual report completed in time

Personal
- having my purse stolen
- seeing my first grey hair
- car accident
- forgetting my birthday/our anniversary
- continuing put-downs from.......
- press reports on single parents (guilt)
- reports of relief aid in Africa (powerlessness)

Action:..

❑ Engine Running Faults

List the areas in your lifestyle and relationships where you are aware that you still experience a lack of personal power, for example:
- meetings
- misunderstandings and confrontations with friends
- sexual relationships
- telephone conversations with my mother
- shop sales assistants.

Action:..

❑ Cooling System

Have you kept cool under the pressure of the last year? Have you been monitoring your stress levels and using the relaxation techniques (pages 91-3)? Note how you may be sabotaging your attempts to bring adequate healing calm and peace into your life.

- not being organized enough
- bringing home work every weekend
- not having enough time with...............
- not having my own private space in the house
- keeping my office door open all the time
- telephone ringing too often

Action:..

❑ Battery Levels

How are your levels of energy at the moment? Have they been as good as could be expected throughout the past year? If not, note what may have been depleting these, for example:

- trying to juggle too much
- trying to please too many people
- not getting enough sleep
- drinking too much
- not going to the gym as often as I need to.

Action:..

❑ Fuel Consumption

How is your body functioning? Is it working efficiently enough for you? Have you been attending to its needs as well as you could? Note some of the ways you may have been (and may be still?!) neglecting it or abusing it, for example:

- putting off going to the dentist
- hoping your backache would just go away
- taking the indigestion or headache tablets but avoiding looking at the underlying cause of these conditions
- putting up with odd aches and pains that ought to be investigated

– not taking vitamin supplements.

Action:...

❏ Steering

Have you been focused enough during the past year? Do you feel you are still going in the right direction? Do you need to re-route yourself in any way? Have you slipped into any bad steering habits, such as:
- following anyone else's lead too much
- sticking to the safe road
- rationalizing about changing your plans
- being reluctant to change direction because of what other people may think.

Action:...

❏ Exhaust Emission

Have you been letting off steam when you need to? Have you been allowing yourself tears when you need to shed them? Have you been cleaning the 'debris' out of your life as you go along through the year, such as:
- a working schedule that is too cluttered with administration
- wasting too much time sitting in traffic jams
- not playing squash anymore
- not shedding a tear even when...........died.

Action:...

❏ Body Work

Take a long hard look at yourself in the mirror and assess what you see. Is there any aspect of your personal appearance that needs attention? How about other aspects of your image? Do you still give an impression to the outside world that you are someone who is worthy of high regard? Note some aspects of your image which you would like to improve,

such as:
- my hair needs re-styling
- I'm heavier than I was last year
- my briefcase is tatty
- the house could do with a coat of paint
- our company logo is beginning to look dated.

Action:...

❑ Driving Companions

How are your relationships, both at home and at work? Are you mixing with the kind of people who help you to feel good about yourself? Do you share the same values with the company you are working for? Have your friends been as supportive/stimulating/fun as you would like them to be? Have you made any new friends? Are you moaning inwardly about any aspects of your relationships? Has anything happened during the last year which is an indication that a relationship may be damaging your self esteem, such as:
- arguments with.........never seem to get resolved
- ....seems to be avoiding me
- we were not consulted about the new bonus scheme (again!)
- no one seems to be taking lunch breaks together anymore
- the children rarely seem to want to share meals with us now.

Action:...

❑ Driving Conditions

Have these been generally favourable for your self esteem this year? Or has it felt like an uphill struggle all the way? What have been the main obstructions in the path of your personal development, success and happiness – for example:
- threat of redundancy hanging over me for the last

three months
- the children seem to be at a 'difficult' age and I am not 'getting through' to them
- recession has hit my productivity
- the competition has quadrupled in the last six months
- every new person I meet is married
- we are too short-staffed
- we've been struggling to pay off debt this year.

Action:...

REMINDER – don't forget to act on your resolutions!

8

Crash Strategy

When searching for a second-hand car, I am always heavily warned by my knowledgeable friends to keep well away from any model that I suspect has been in a crash. So I dutifully scour the service history and look suspiciously at every little tell-tale scratch and bump. My cynicism soars if I am told a car has been off the road for a while. I don't want to hear about the owner's ill-health or posting to outer Mongolia for six months. I find my interest moving on and then, should I come across another dubious example, panic begins to set in. I start to think that the only answer is to mortgage myself to a brand new vehicle which I neither want nor need.

I have to admit that the problem feels even worse if the owner admits to a crash and assures me the car has had expert attention and is now fully recovered. I begin to get distraught – I admire the owner for his or her honesty but I still do not feel in any way inclined to buy the car. As I guiltily turn my back on these honourable sellers, the mechanics among you will probably breathe a sigh of relief on my behalf. After all, you must have gathered by now that I haven't a hope of distinguishing the most proficiently executed repair from a con-man's patch-up.

But my comfort is that, in the people-hunting business, I am likely to have a head start on most of you! My field is much wider because I do not have to narrow my choice down to the perfect 'stories' or CVs. If I suspect that someone's self esteem has been 'through a rough patch', I give them a chance simply because I have some idea of how they should be functioning in their recovered state and what kind of emotional repair work they need to do. I am aware that most people cannot afford to be so magnanimous when they are searching for the 'right person'; I can understand their fear because I know that without the wisdom I have gained from recovering from my own serious 'crashes' and my subsequent professional training, I would be just as keen to find someone with a clean bill of emotional health, whether I were searching for a teacher for my children, a doctor to do my operation, a childminder to look after my baby or even someone to share my bed!

But just as I miss out on gaining pleasure from driving the wonderful bargains to be found in the veteran market, so others miss out by avoiding people who have recovered from emotional crises. In fact, I believe that they may be missing out on much more than I do, because while I'm not sure whether it is possible for a car to be stronger after a crash, I am convinced that people *can* be!

Is the answer then to go forth and seek a self esteem crisis in the hope that it will guide you towards superior psychological strength? No, of course not – that would be as crazy as driving a shaky car into a brick wall, just as an experiment. And although most people realize the foolishness of kicking a car that won't start, many still feel the urge to do just that (that famous scene in *Fawlty Towers* when Basil Fawlty rips down a branch of a tree to 'beat a lesson' into his ailing car is hilarious partly because we can all identify with his feelings). We still live in an age where too many people think that bashing the living confidence out of someone will eventually 'toughen them up'. As I grew up in stoical Great Britain, in the aftermath of two wars when the 'spare the rod spoil the child' philosophy was at one of its heights, I have seen plenty of evidence of the crippling effects of this sort of craziness. Sometimes it seems to me that the country is crawling with beings in steely confident shells that encase a quivering mass of self-loathing within!

There is no doubt that our national habit of whipping wimps and humbling the would-be heroes breeds a people who stalwartly thrive on the minor bumps in life. But what happens when they are confronted with a ten-ton lorry-load of trouble such as a redundancy *and* a marriage failure? The sad truth is that they often crumble into deep depression and are all too ready to assign themselves to the scrap heap. Many unfortunately never manage to climb out of their deep despair, simply because they do not know it is possible to do so. So however much of a hero they may have been in the past, when the big crunch comes they may not even attempt repair. It's no wonder that we British are so suspicious and intolerant of anyone showing a hint of low self esteem!

It isn't the ordeal itself of a self esteem crisis that can give survivors that extra strength, but the experience of working through a good-quality recovery process.

As with the healing of other emotional wounds, when we have a self esteem crash we need therefore to do more than just 'sit it out' – we have to take constructive steps to ensure that we receive the very best quality emotional repair – the kind designed to reinforce our psychological foundations and not just 'touch-up' our outer shell.

I sincerely hope that you will never need to use the following strategy, but I know that the chances are that most of us will. However carefully we maintain our self esteem there will always be the danger of major humbling experiences that will leave it very badly dented indeed.

◇ Exercise: Devising My Own Personal Crash Strategy

As you are reading through this strategy you will come across questions to ask yourself. Each is marked with a small box to tick or mark with a cross.

✔ Step 1: Take Out Your 999 File

This vital file, of course, will have already been placed in a readily available spot (e.g. a section in your diary or a file on your computer or in your desk). It will contain the contact numbers for the people you may need to help you get your self esteem back on the road.

There is a saying that you only get to know who your real friends are when you are in trouble. This is even more true when the trouble is to do with self esteem. Unless you have thought through carefully *the kind of friend you need in need*, you can find yourself surrounded by people riding haughtily around on high horses telling you that *they* would never have sunk down to your needy level!

Towing Service

A 'no-nonsense' friend who'll give you practical help during the aftermath without asking questions or making emotional demands on you. The help you require to 'tow' you along for a short while will obviously depend on the kind of problem which has hit you. You could, for example, need:

- babysitting
- voluntary secretarial help
- someone to stand in for you at a meeting
- someone to make telephone calls to difficult customers
- lifts
- help with shopping.

Ambulance

A friend who is willing and able to give you some TLC ('Tender Loving Care' for you novices at self-nurturing!). Again this kind of help will vary according to the size of the problem and your preferences, but it could include:

- endless chats over cups of freshly brewed quality tea or coffee
- a bed and a high-quality diet for a few days
- back massage
- a big hug.

Police

Another no-nonsense friend, but one who is strong enough to stay around and give you protection as long as you need it. When our self esteem is in crisis it is amazing how incapable we become at self-defence. Every scrap of learning on self-protective skills seems to vanish from our minds. This friend will be there until you can cope on your own. For example, you might need them to:

- have a word with nosy neighbours or colleagues
- speak to your boss on your behalf
- liaise with your union
- guard you from the press.

Solicitor

A level-headed friend who will help you to *think through* any action you may need to take and who will remind you of your rights. When our self esteem is low we often think it is not worth the trouble to stand up for our rights. Alternatively, there is a danger that we feel so powerless that we 'lash out' in all directions and do things we may regret later. This friend could help you to:

- identify your legal and moral rights
- write an assertive script (see pages 85-8)
- prepare your Fogging responses to destructive critics (page 79-81)
- role-play, taking the part of Devil's Advocate
- prepare your case before meeting a real solicitor!

Insurance Agent

A friend who can (and will!) dip into his or her pocket to help you out if you should require some emergency funding. It should be someone with whom you can have a business-like arrangement, who will give you the money (or other resources) in a way which doesn't dent your self esteem further. You can often recognize a person's ability to do this by the tone of his or her voice, which tends to be very flat, brisk and business-like whenever the subject is discussed. When you are receiving, you should not be made to feel like a needy, grateful charity – you should feel as though the other person is just 'doing a simple job that needs to be done'. The kind of help you may temporarily need might include:

- money for a holiday
- a cheque for a course of counselling or therapy
- the loan of an office and its contents
- share of a nanny
- a house to live in
- a car to drive.

❏ Write the Contact List for Your 999 File

But first, to avoid setting yourself up for disappointment, please note:

1. Some friends might be able to do several jobs but rarely can even a saint do all of them.
2. It's a good idea to put aside notions about being loyal to 'best friends' or hurting someone's feelings. You need, and deserve, the best person available for each 'job'.
3. Your selection should not be based on irrelevant criteria such as 'He owes me a favour' (he might not agree by the time you need help!) or 'She ought to be good at that, it's

her job' (she may not feel like taking a 'busman's holiday').

4. It's a good idea to check beforehand with your friends about whether they feel willing and able to be on your list and to take on the role for which you need them!

My 999 Contact Numbers of Friends for my personal Recovery Service:

1. Towing Service.......................................
2. Ambulance...
3. Police...
4. Solicitor...
5. Insurance Agent.....................................

✔ Step 2: Dial, Write or Shout for Help

This may sound simple, but for people with low self esteem it might be the hardest part of the crash to tolerate! Even if we have a brilliant 999 File, when we are in the black pit of self-hatred we can be utterly convinced that we don't deserve help, or that no one will *want* to help us, or that it will 'do us good' to suffer through on our own!

If these kinds of irrational thoughts begin to creep in, you need to demolish them quickly with some appropriate affirmations.

❑ **Compose three affirmations by completing these sentences:**

'I deserve help because...'
'I have a right to be helped because...'
'Someone would want to help me because...'

✔ Step 3: Take Yourself Off the Road for a While

Ideally I would recommend a spell in a health farm, but few of us can afford this. Nevertheless there are many less costly ways of giving yourself the same kind of recuperative care. Low self esteem plays havoc with our bodies, so it is really important to make sure that you give yourself some *extra* physical nurturing. You will also need to find some way of stilling your mind, which will no doubt be very restless and full of obsessional thoughts. Some time spent in a peaceful location might help – at the very least find a place to do some meditation (pages 92-3).

❑ **Note how you could provide yourself with some** *immediate* **'time out' and some extra nurturing, in the event of a self esteem crash.**

✔ Step 4: Give Yourself a Dose of Positive Thinking and Positive Experiences

As I said earlier, it is so easy to write off not just yourself when your self esteem is low, but also the entire world! After a crash, it's not a good idea to rely on your usual warning signals that you are creeping back into a negative rut – just assume that you are and take action!

If you are short of ideas, you could perhaps re-read the section on positive thinking (pages 66-8), but you may also need some extra positive thinking literature to help you through this stage (see the Further Reading chapter).

❑ **List some activities you could readily engage in to help recover your positive frame of mind.**

✔ Step 5: Do Your Emotional Repair Work ASAP

By working methodically through the Emotional Healing stages in this book you might be able to do a very effective DIY job, but if you do not feel up to it don't hesitate to seek professional help from a counsellor or therapist. It is a good idea to gather information about the services available in your area so that you do not have to do this in a panic when you are at a desperate stage. My best advice on finding a suitable person or agency to help you is to ask around for the recommendations of 'satisfied customers'. The best advice is likely to come from those whose values are similar to your own. Unfortunately a therapist's fees and the string of letters after his or her name are not necessarily good guides as to whether or not that person will be of use to you – especially for the purposes of helping you through this kind of crisis.

If you are likely to be short of money, there are usually ways and means of getting some free counselling. Your doctor or library should be able to give you local contact lists; relevant professional associations are also usually able to provide you with a list of local qualified practitioners.

❏ **Note down the names and numbers of professionally trained people whom you could go to for help should this be necessary.**

✔ Step 6: Check the Map and Your Route Plan

Any kind of crash is tough to work through, but when you have become a veteran survivor like me you also know that catastrophe can offer amazing opportunities for change and growth. I look back at most of the life-crises that sent me hurtling into my black ditches and now think 'Thank goodness! Without that experience I would still have been driving down that old road!'

So seize the fluidity of the crisis situation and review your journey. This could be the time for a new job, a new relationship, a change of direction or destination, a new driving style and so on!

❑ **Note down your favourite life-planning and personal change exercises, books, cassettes or other aids you could keep handy to use as you work towards the end of your recovery.**

✔ Step 7: Join a Classic Car Club

If you have worked effectively and finished your emotional healing, you should be able to drive off on your own confidently (but still cautiously). I can assure you, though, that you will have much more fun and reduce your chances of further crashes if you have the support of fellow-survivors.

Reaching the very depths of despair that a crash of self

esteem brings and working through this kind of survival strategy is a very special experience. And while, as you know, I am not in favour of 'personally developed élites', I do know that there is so much we can gain from meeting regularly with people who can empathize. This is especially important during your early days back on the road. Being in a self-help group can, for example, help you to release feelings safely, share tips and gain many more numbers for your 999 File. But even more importantly, together you can celebrate all your successes in style! How about an international rally with golden trophies for self esteem success stories?!

❏ **Note who should attend your rally and who should present you with your prize!**

Full esteem ahead!

Section 4
Using Your Strength to Empower

9

Building Self Esteem in Others

Helping other people grow can become life's greatest joy.
ALAN LOY McGINNIS

Let's assume that you have successfully worked through your own self esteem building programme and feel great about yourself and excited about your life ahead. According to my theory, you should now be aching to read the contents of this chapter! You will be finding yourself, quite naturally, pulled in the direction of helping others feel good about themselves, not because this is something you feel you *ought* to do, but because you *want* to. In fact, in my experience it is by no means unusual for many people at this stage of their personal development to start asking questions about counselling and psychotherapy courses.

I am convinced that this attraction towards my line of business is fuelled by genuine concern for others, as much of my work takes place in groups and I can see the evidence of their caring in action. But I do admit that the interest is not entirely altruistic in its nature. People often openly admit that part of the appeal of my kind of job is that it appears to be so satisfying and rewarding. I would certainly not dispute this observation because I can honestly say that I rank the tears of joy which I feel on hearing of the happiness and success of clients among the most powerful 'peak experiences' of my life.

But is the only option becoming a professional helper? Certainly not. Indeed, while I appreciate that becoming a professional might be the right way ahead for a few, I feel that it is our everyday relationships and roles that can have *most* impact on the growth of other people's self esteem. I am confident that if we were all to make better use of these opportunities there would be very much less need for people to train for my kind of job. I have no doubt that a hunt for an alternative way of earning my bread and butter would be a small price to pay for the pleasure and stimulation I would gain from living in a society which routinely enhanced each individual's self-worth.

So, in the charitable pursuit of my own redundancy I have written this chapter! I hope it will give you some ideas on how you can use and develop your personal power to help build the self esteem, not just of your nearest and dearest and your colleagues, but also of the butcher, the baker and the candle-stick maker!

First we will take a look at some of the characteristics self esteem builders commonly share, and will note how these are translated into everyday behaviour in three common roles: The Manager, the Parent and the Citizen. Secondly, I will introduce a short step-by-step personal development programme to strengthen your own self esteem building capacities.

What Kind of Person Builds Others' Self Esteem?

I am sure you have met, as indeed I have, a number of people who seem to ooze self esteem building vibrations out of every pore. The minute they walk into the room we can feel our self-worth growing. Equally there are people whose very presence seems to make us feel destined to remain the size of an ant for ever.

The following is a list of characteristics which I have often observed when the first kind of person is relating to others in either personal or public life.

Profile of a Self Esteem Builder

Generally, people who consistently help others to feel good about themselves:

- are proud of their own high level of self esteem
  - *but* do not set themselves up as perfect beings who have arrived at the finishing post of their own self-improvement.
- are happy, successful and optimistic about the future
  - *but* haven't forgotten the pain of their past, and use it openly to empathize with (and not judge) the current suffering and depression of others.
- are open-minded and obviously genuinely interested in hearing new ideas and meeting and understanding new people
  - *but* clearly demand their right to maintain a firm ethical framework for themselves and any groups for which they have responsibility.
- believe passionately in the ability of people and organizations to change
  - *but* remain respectful of others' fears and anxieties and do not abuse their power to pressurize people aggressively unless they perceive the status quo to be grossly unjust.
- take immense pleasure in getting to know and nurture the individual character and potential of each person in any group or organization

   – *but* do not lose sight of the power and needs of everyone
     as a whole.
- are highly generous, not just with their money but also with
their resources, time and wisdom
   – *but* firmly reserve their right to keep ample reserves of
     each for their own self-sustenance and protection.
- are generally calm, controlled, patient and trustful in their
relationships
   – *but* make it clear that they will never knowingly allow
     themselves (or those they want to protect) to be abused
     or 'taken for a ride'.

But now let's come down to earth and see how these paragons
are likely to behave in their everyday lives. I have chosen three
common roles (Manager, Parent and Citizen) to use as illustrations. As you read the following lists, think of people you
know who are (at least relatively) good examples of each type,
because they could become very useful role-models. (But
remember that the aim of this exercise is to raise your
awareness and gather useful tips, not to make you feel
inadequate and guilty – you should be resistant to that kind of
'rubbish' by now anyway!)

Self Esteem Building Managers

In the course of their everyday lives, these are the type of
people who:

- frequently leave their ivory towers and become actively and
co-operatively involved at 'shop-floor' or fieldwork level
- greet staff warmly, using individuals' names, and show an
interest in each person's background, special interests and
life outside the organization
- use non-verbal behaviour which indicates respect (e.g. they
do not intrude on others' personal space by touching
unnecessarily; they maintain direct eye-contact but do not

stare others down; they rise when someone comes into the room; they rearrange office furniture to less depowering positions)

- notice the health of staff and take a keen interest in ensuring that fair pay reviews and safety and welfare provisions are given a priority
- regularly ask for feedback about job satisfaction, and ask for (and reward) constructive suggestions for improvements
- show genuine delight when even a junior displays superior skill or knowledge
- delegate courageously without breathing heavily down the neck of those given responsibility for their 'pet projects'
- openly share responsibility for mistakes, and never look for scapegoats
- suspend judgement after failures until objective 'post-mortems' have been organized (designed to facilitate 'hindsight learning' rather than blame and punishment)
- hold lively meetings which are structured in a way that allows everyone the chance to contribute appropriately
- give presentations and write reports/memos/instructions, etc. in language that is free from jargon and can be easily understood by all levels of ability and experience
- set inspiring targets which are challenging to individual potential but still highly achievable and unlikely to damage team spirit
- openly appreciate (and amply reward) the efforts and dedication of those members of staff who do the boring or least 'glamorous' tasks
- promptly and directly criticize unacceptable behaviour and performance, but at the same time make constructive suggestions on how the required standards can be achieved
- use a strong angry 'arm' to deal quickly with bullying, racist or sexist behaviour and discriminatory practices
- acknowledge the rights of staff to refuse overtime if the work intrudes on their personal life
- oversee just and meaningful appraisal sessions
- involve staff at all levels in appropriate aspects of strategic

planning sessions
- take an interest in keeping organizational hierarchy as flat and flexible as possible to allow power and responsibility genuinely to be shared
- ensure that office accommodation is planned with the comfort and pleasure of staff in mind as well as economy and efficiency
- listen sympathetically to the needs of staff who require flexible working arrangements (to look after dependents or to work through personal crises)
- provide adequate practical and emotional support during periods of high stress and transition
- join in regular celebrations of triumphs and achievements
- set aside time to act as an encouraging mentor and guide for new and junior staff and students, and openly share the secrets of their own success and high self esteem
- ensure that training and personal development programmes are given high priority, adequate funding and designed in consultation with staff
- give departing staff a respectful and appreciative farewell.

Self Esteem Building Parents

We can recognize these parents because they are the ones who:

- say frequently not only 'I love you' but also 'I like you because...'
- squat down to their children's level so their sheer size and height are not overpowering
- use language that can be easily understood but do not 'baby' or patronize their children
- listen calmly and attentively to children's inarticulately recounted stories, explanations and fantasies
- are fascinated and thrilled by a child's demonstration of personal qualities and aptitudes which are different from

their own
- give lots of hugs and kisses but hold back (without showing offence) when their children want some physical distance
- tell their children how much they have enriched their life and how much they have learned from them
- make unconditional promises to their children that they will look after them until they are fully able to fend for themselves
- provide a home that is, in its layout and decor, child- as well as adult-centred
- make an effort to respond to each child's needs separately, not following blind rules and strategies for bringing up 'the kids'
- discipline by rewards for good behaviour, rarely using punishment
- encourage each child to reflect his or her individuality (e.g. in terms of clothing/room decoration/choice of presents/choice of school subjects and career/choice of friends)
- plan and defend the right to have periods of quality time with their children
- engage in leisure activities and holidays that are designed for their children's pleasure as well as their own recuperation and stimulation
- encourage children to look after themselves, taking time to teach them the life-skills they need to be self-nurturing and independent
- ask for (but do not demand) appropriate help from their children
- praise children for effort and small improvements as well as major achievements
- ask their children for their opinions and views, and listen with respect and interest even though these views may differ from their own
- support them in disappointments and hurts (however trivial) and let them express their feelings as freely as possible
- demonstrate their trust by frequently letting their children take calculated risks and learn from their own mistakes

- involve children in their adult world rather than making them keep a guarded distance (e.g. including them in conversations/taking them into work sometimes/having social gatherings for all ages)
- say 'I don't know' and 'I'm sorry' rather than pretending that they have all the answers or are always right

Self Esteem Building Citizens

We can recognize these people because in their everyday lives we might, for example, expect to see them:

- smile and say 'Good morning' to strangers as well as friends whom they meet regularly en route to and from work or while they are out shopping
- say friendly, courteous ' Hellos' and 'Good-byes' to people making deliveries to their home or office
- make an effort (even if not always successful!) to get to know and use people's names
- patiently (but not patronizingly) engage in uninspiring 'small talk' to help put people less socially skilled than themselves at ease
- answer the phone in a way that gives the impression that the caller is human
- welcome (and show a respectful interest in) new arrivals to their neighbourhood
- lend (within reason!) their material possessions, or offer access to their land when others may be in need of them
- engage (sometimes anonymously) in small acts of neighbourly kindness (e.g. checking if an elderly person's milk has been taken indoors, or watching out for lurking strangers when neighbours are away)
- keep the exterior of their home, and their garden, in a state that indicates a show of respect and consideration for the community
- take care to dispose of their litter and not damage property

which is used and valued by others
- wait patiently while a disabled or elderly person enters a train or bus or checks out at a supermarket
- give up their seat in a train or bus to someone who may obviously find standing a strain
- give time and/or money to help people who are less able or less financially fortunate than themselves
- take care to make sure that communal buildings feel welcoming and accessible to all people
- share their professional knowledge with others who would never be able to have the same training and education
- say thank-you to people who give generously of their time and services even when they have been paid adequately
- write letters of appreciation to people and organizations offering public services which are often taken for granted
- make an effort to understand and accommodate the needs and wishes of people from differing cultures, generations and religions
- refuse to participate in malicious gossip and rumour
- show disdain for humour which hurts or puts down others who do not have the power to defend themselves
- assertively counter racist or sexist language when they hear it being used
- drive their cars in a way which shows concern for the needs and wishes of others on and off the road
- use environmentally-friendly products even when they are not in their own home town
- show concern for the needs of other people's children at parents' meetings at school, or for fellow patients' interests in hospital even when they know they themselves are being discharged
- support projects designed to protect the safety of children, the disabled or elderly even though they themselves may be young, childless or able-bodied.
- speak up for the rights and interests of people who cannot defend themselves
- campaign against unjust and discriminatory legislation, rules and practices even when these do not directly concern

them
- vote for, and support, politicians who have the personal power and commitment to put democratic theory into practice
- keep informed and encourage debate about important community and world issues even though they may have a comfortable lifestyle themselves

Hopefully, reading the above has left you in a state of inspiration and excitement, but no doubt it has also started you thinking critically about your own behaviour. If you feel quite satisfied that your own everyday behaviour could match the above examples, read no further – just carry on the good work! But if you would like to strengthen your self esteem building capacities, here are some practical personal development steps you could take.

Step 1: Analyse Your Current Strengths

This is our usual first step and will help you to plan an effective programme for yourself because you will know just how much time you may need to devote to this aspect of your personal development.

◇ Exercise – Assessing My Current Self Esteem Building Strength

1. Take a moment to bring to mind some examples of self esteem builders you know of.
   In your imagination, place them together in one corner of

a large room. Watch them interacting.

2. Now imagine that in the other corner there are a number people who habitually, either intentionally or unintention- ally, seem to diminish people's sense of worth (I am sure that if you yourself have had a self esteem problem you will have many examples to draw on!).

    Watch this group interact for a moment.

3. Now imagine some visitors coming into the room. Where do they seem inclined to go? How are they greeted by each group? Use your mind's eye to watch everyone's verbal and non-verbal behaviour.

4. Now freeze the scene and imagine that *you* are walking into this room. You must position yourself somewhere in relation to the two different groups. Carefully choose a spot which would be indicative of your own *current* self esteem building capacities – with most people most of the time!

Did you find this exercise easy? If you managed to visualize the scene, did you find yourself pacing up and down between the two groups, or did you want to turn your back and run? No doubt your self esteem building qualities, like those of most people, have a tendency to ebb and flow. Some days I know that I would feel quite at home with the paragons, while on other days I might feel uncomfortably close to the 'baddies'. I also know that I tend to be consistently empowering with some people, but that there are others who always seem to see the least caring side of me. Unless we want to leave the human race and apply for canonization, that's how I suppose it will always be to *some extent*. Nevertheless, if you want to become more like the self esteem builders *most* of the time, plan *now* to set aside some time to work through the next five steps. In the mean time, make sure that you spend as much time as you can with good role-models, and keep observing and noting the helpful aspects of their behaviour.

Step 2: Firm Up Your Resistance to Temptation

In the Introduction to this book we looked briefly at the staggering price both individuals and their societies can pay for low self esteem. The cost is so phenomenal that a visitor from another planet would no doubt be utterly staggered to see a society routinely condoning and often actively encouraging such self-destructive behaviour. Being strangers to 'human nature', they would find it difficult to understand why we are so easily tempted by the *short- term rewards* which low self esteem behaviour so evidently often offers.

But fallible we are, and I am sure that every honest reader will admit to being seduced by the charms of others' low self esteem at some time or other. The following chart is designed to help firm up your resolve to resist encouraging other people in their low self esteem, by reminding you of the long-term damage that can result from playing these enticing 'games'.

THE LONG-TERM EFFECTS
OF LOW SELF ESTEEM BEHAVIOUR
1. Seductive Low Self Esteem Behaviour 2. Short-Term Gains

3. Long-Term Effects

1. Seductive Low Self Esteem Behaviour	2. Short-Term Gains	3. Long-Term Effects
1. Fawning/Grovelling (such as people who 'suck up' to teacher or 'butter up' the boss; guru worshippers; 'blind' lovers)	**2.** If we're on the receiving end, we feel flattered and more important and get a shot of 'phoney' self esteem	**3.** The idols and 'adored ones' get bored and irritated. They lose respect for the fawners and then reject them or become aggressive (thus damaging their own self esteem!)

1. Inhibition and Restraint (such as the unassertive who hold back their opinions at meetings, who won't interfere, complain or 'rock the boat'; those who let others take the lead and smile at queue jumpers)

2. We can make quick decisions and complete more tasks speedily by letting these types take a back seat

3. Many good ideas and useful criticisms are lost, so quality and innovation suffer (e.g. politicians whose policies are out of date and companies who are producing unwanted, shoddy goods)

1. Playing 'Stupid' or 'Helpless' (such as 'damsels in distress'; perpetual seekers of unnecessary advice)

2. If called upon for this kind of help, we bask in the glory of hero/ heroine worship

3. The heroic and clever 'rescuers' and 'gurus' burn out from taking too much responsibility, and get sick and lonely on their pedestals (like the 'head of the family' who doesn't know his or her children, or the friendless executive who dies a premature, unmourned death)

1. Submissiveness/ Over-politeness and Conformity (such as the 'no trouble' child; the obedient 'cog in the working wheel'; the smiling household slave)

2. We live and work in a peaceful atmosphere and the future feels predictable

3. Resentment builds up and suddenly (and uncontrollably) bursts out from 'under the carpet' in the form of aggressive rebellion (e.g. 'difficult' adolescents; mutinous workers; bitter militant uprisings of the oppressed)

1. Do-gooding (e.g. people-pleasers who unnecessarily give service day and night; altruistic artisans who under-charge for goods; volunteers who run services which should, and could, be paid for; workers who willingly sacrifice their time off to ensure a job is finished)

2. We reap the material rewards of cheap cheerful labour

3. The helped feel too guilty and ashamed to enjoy their success and wealth; over-dependence on do-gooders leads to difficulty surviving when they leave or get burnt out (such as the miserable millionaire who cannot enjoy his/her 'ill-gotten' gains; the incapable widower of the 'good wife'; or the voluntary organization which grinds to a halt when its key 'martyr to the cause' gets sick)

1. Readily Assuming and Absorbing Guilt (such as willing scapegoats who take the blame immediately any problem emerges; people who say 'sorry' when someone else has knocked *them* in the street; the bullied child who thinks he or she 'deserves' it; the obsequious secretary taking blame for his or her boss's error; those who make false confessions to protect loved ones; the silent battered wife; the victim of incest from a beloved adult)

2. These people may allow us to get away with no punishment or blame for our mistakes

3. Bullying and other unjust practices can become accepted as normal and may even become institutionalized. Motivation to be considerate or fair or to do careful and efficient work is reduced. A 'big mistake' can occur (as with inefficient accounting which plunges a company 'into the red'; a victim who gets badly hurt or killed; an over-indulged child who secretly turns to drugs; the over-worked Social Service workers who fail to check an 'at risk' family; the jailing or execution of innocent people)

◇ Exercise: Dealing with Temptation

1. Read the list (remembering that it is not definitive, and summoning up every ounce of honesty within you). Note down examples of when you yourself have fallen for the temptation of encouraging similar low self esteem behaviour. Note also what negative results there were, or could have been.
2. If possible, share the above with a friend or sympathetic colleague. Be clear that your friend's task is *not* to 'hear confession and give forgiveness' but simply to discuss with you some constructive ideas on how you can resist similar temptations in the future.

For example:

- **re: over-conformity** – ask for more constructive criticism; pay for an Assertiveness Training programme for your company or for a particular individual.
- **re: inhibition** – ensure that everyone has a turn to speak at (work or family) meetings; initiate an easy-to-use complaints procedure.
- **re: do-gooding** – pay for services (if only by donation to a charity) which you believe should and could be paid for
- **re: playing helpless** – refuse to help even if it means you have to wait and put up with the 'helpless' person's whining.

Step 3: Take Control of Your Prejudices

We tend to think of prejudice as something nasty lurking in the minds of people who are selfish and narrow-minded. It is often excruciatingly difficult for those who are sincerely concerned with boosting the esteem of others to admit to being tainted with negative biases towards certain people. But like it or not we are *all* riddled with psychological baggage (acquired in even the most 'respectable' environments!) which predisposes us to take a more favourable attitude towards some people than others. Pushing our uncomfortable attitudes into the back recesses of our minds can only enhance their power to damage our attempts to help people. The danger is that (at their best!) these prejudices may surface, without our realizing it, from our unconscious as patronizing or rationalized rejecting behaviour.

Perhaps the most difficult prejudices to deal with are those that are firmly embedded in our general culture and have also been reinforced by an emotional personal experience. These experiences lead us to become convinced that we are acting in the interests of the other person – when we are in fact damaging their self esteem.

Let's look at some examples of 'well-meaning' behaviour which are obviously very different from blatant prejudice such as racist or sexist remarks, but which nevertheless carry subtle put-downs.

1. Well-meaning behaviour – *'How exciting – well done! Considering that you've been brought up by a family of bankers, you're achievement is particularly amazing.'*	2. Denied prejudicial belief – *all bankers are boring and pedantic.*	3. Possible root cause – *experience of living with a dull bank manager for a father, reinforced by a general cultural belief about bankers.*
1. *'I know you had your heart set on working directly with customers, but as you have such a wonderfully strong voice I think for your sake it would be best if you worked in telephone sales. You would not be making the best use of your strengths working in the field.'*	2. Denied prejudice – *people with loud voices should never be face-to-face with customers.*	3. Possible root cause – *personal 'horror' anecdote about a lost contract told by a revered trainer on a management course, reinforced by the cultural belief that a loud voice in a woman is unattractive.*

1. 'You do an amazing job and I can't fault your performance, but isn't it about time you began to take things a little easier? I know you are very fit and you love your job, but don't you think you deserve a quieter life now?' (Said soon after a friend has just turned 60)

2. Denied prejudice – *all over-60s are less physically fit and less capable of doing their job than they were when they were when they were 59!*

3. Possible root cause – *cultural attitudes towards the elderly and a fixed national retirement age, fed by personal experience of beloved parents who grew old 'before their years'.*

I do not believe there is any quick, easy way of ridding ourselves of these kinds of prejudices; for most of us it is better to think in terms of *taking more control* over them. We can do this chiefly through regularly asking assertively and courageously for honest feedback and constructive appraisal from those who are receiving our help, or at least from others who can be trusted to be objective observers of our behaviour. But, as anyone who has done some basic counselling training knows, we can help make ourselves more generally open-minded by taking some of the actions which I suggest in the next exercise.

◇ Exercise – Extending My Empathy Horizons

Try these few ways of developing your empathy – *then*, why not experiment with making up some further exercises for yourself? These could, for example, help you become more understanding of the specific people you are trying to help.

1. Over the next week, buy yourself three different newspapers from the ones which you usually read. Mark the stories, articles or quotes which bring out the 'critic' response in you (e.g. 'I wish they wouldn't

always...'/'People shouldn't...'/'The trouble with the world today is...', etc.)

2. Watch two TV programmes which you 'hate' while at the same time imagining that you are someone who would really appreciate them. Make every effort to enjoy them and see the positive aspects of these programmes.

3. Choose someone whom you would like to help with his or her self esteem and reflect on how this person *might* have spent the last week. Write an imaginary personal journal for this person for the past week, noting how he or she may have reacted not only to personal events but also to the news, the weather, etc. Then, if possible, set aside a time to chat to this person about the week and note how accurate you have been in your attempt to 'step into his or her shoes'. If you are at all surprised, share your feelings (for example: 'I didn't realize you were feeling so fed-up/liked that kind of music/got on so well with...') and discuss. Later, reflect and try to figure out whether your 'inaccurate' empathy was caused more by the other person's non-communicativeness or a presupposition on your part.

4. Share with several people (whom you can trust to talk to you with honesty) mutual first impressions. If together you have revealed any initial prejudices, discuss the possible causes for your pre-judgements and how they have been corrected.

Step 4: Improve Your Listening Skills

This is perhaps the most crucial step of all. An ability to listen well to others is the single most important characteristic of self esteem builders. Many people think that all you need to do to be a good listener is to keep your own mouth shut. This may be so if the people who are doing the talking are highly amusing, positive, energetic, charismatic, skilled and confident orators. But are most of the people you know with low self esteem like this? No, the truth is that they are usually the opposite. Cruel as this sounds, if we keep our mouth shut too tightly in their company the chances are either that we'll drop off or they'll dry up!

Low self esteem can have a devastatingly negative effect on the articulacy and tone of our voices. I know that when mine is at one of its lower ebbs I mumble and fumble elongated, unedited sentences, making it impossibly hard for even my nearest and dearest to fathom out what I want. I also know that other people's articulacy is affected in a different way. Some find that when their self-worth is shaky they can only screech out in monosyllables, while others become literally 'dumb-struck'.

So, contrary to popular belief, the key to listening well is not endless sympathetic patience but active participation! Below I have listed some tips from the world of counselling training. You could use these as a checklist to monitor and improve your own skills.

TIPS ON HOW TO LISTEN ENCOURAGINGLY TO PEOPLE WITH LOW SELF ESTEEM

- If you have a limited time available, say clearly (before they start to talk if possible) how much time you have, then take responsibility for ending the conversation (it does not help anyone's self-worth to be granted a begrudging half-ear).
- Hold back on interrupting with your 'own story' (for example: 'Oh, the same thing happened to me when...' or 'Gosh, I've never been there...')
- If you are talking face-to-face, try to maintain some direct eye-contact, but do not stare. The amount of contact you can expect will depend of course on the cultural background of the person talking. For example, when talking to someone from most Western cultures you would be aiming for about 50 per cent eye-contact, but with those from some Eastern cultures that amount would be perceived as intimidating. If you are finding the lack of eye-contact distracting, say so – because people with low self esteem are often unaware of their eye-roving habits (for example, say 'I'm finding it difficult to concentrate on what you are saying while you are looking around').
- Don't patronize by leaning forward too much, nor threaten by moving too near. People with low self esteem often feel more comfortable surrounded by a greater area of personal space than most. Even if you are on the phone, move yourself into a more upright position (rather than a laid-back, 'I-could-fall-asleep-any-minute-now' one).
- If they are finding it particularly difficult to talk, it sometimes helps to 'mirror' their tone of voice and body position (experienced counsellors with well-developed empathy skills often find themselves doing this automatically).

- Indicate your attention with plenty of nods, grunts or encouraging words ('Um,' 'Really?' 'That's interesting,' etc.)
- Repeat back verbatim their last word or the end of their last sentence, using an appropriate tone ('Manchester!' or '...three reports'). Although this may sound an odd thing to do, it does have the effect of indicating that you are listening attentively, but does not interrupt their flow. If you have never used this technique before (or think you haven't!), watch other good listeners using it before practising yourself.
- After a minute or so, reflect back a summary (by interrupting if you need to) of what you think you have heard them saying ('So it's been a difficult week').
- Ask open rather than closed questions to get them to clarify and expand on what they are saying (for example, asking 'What did you think about that?' or 'How did you feel?' is more useful than limiting the possible response by asking specifically 'Did you get upset?' or 'Was it terrible for you?').
- Use their name occasionally when asking a question or making a comment.
- Every so often, make an empathy statement or ask a question to check out that you have understood their feelings accurately (such as 'That must have irritated you' or 'You sound pleased, were you?')
- Check the message you are receiving against their body language ('I'm puzzled because even though you said very clearly you enjoyed it, you were frowning as you spoke'). Often in their anxiety people with low self esteem unintentionally give out confusing mixed messages.
- Avoid rushing in immediately to rescue silences with 'good' advice, unnecessary reassurances or 'cheer-up' humour. Allow a little time for a 'breather', but not as much as you would normally allow for more confident people who can tolerate silences without panicking. Then encourage them to continue by re-stating a paraphrase of what they have said so far (such as, 'Sounds like the last six

months have been an uphill climb'). Alternatively, without 'accusing' them of a feeling (such as, 'You're embarrassed, aren't you?), make a careful empathic guess at the feeling behind the silence ('I'm wondering if you're finding it a bit embarrassing to talk about this now?').

- If you are going to conclude the conversation (and often you shall have to), do so by summarizing your impression of the whole of what you have heard and, if appropriate, add a final positive appreciative comment (for example: 'I've got a much clearer idea of what is needed now. Thanks for telling me').

◊ Exercise – Improving My Listening Skills

1. Keeping the above checklist to hand, watch several TV programmes or listen to some radio discussions and see if you can spot any of these tips being used. Also note the bad listening habits you observe.
2. Together with a friend, practise your skills by giving each other five minutes to talk on a particular subject and then sharing feedback. If you are feeling courageous, record yourselves, repeating the exercise until you can hear a distinct improvement.

Don't forget that listening is simply a skill which can be learned by anyone – no one is born either a bad or good listener!

Step 5: Improve Your Ability to Give Compliments and Appreciations

Like listening, there is more to giving good positive feedback than meets the eye! Again, a popular misconception tends to rule: people often think that all they have to do is improve the *quantity* of compliments they give out – in fact, doing this can be counter-productive because it often sounds phoney and patronizing.)

Giving Effective Compliments to People with Low Self Esteem

- **Choose an appropriate time and place** – don't slip them into a hurried conversation where they are hardly likely to be noticed or can be easily dismissed. Also, refrain from the temptation to give them a cheering boost when they are obviously in a highly negative mood. You will only end up feeling rejected and they will feel worse for not being able to respond to your kindness! Remember, too, that people with very low self esteem are likely to derive more benefit from compliments given in private. As their self esteem grows you will be able to give more public praise. In some organizations and groups where compliments have traditionally been very scarce, it may be a good idea to initiate a safe, 'approved' time-slot for mutual appreciation sessions (such as starting or ending staff meetings with appropriate thanks to staff members).
- **Try to maintain eye-contact** – though this might be difficult because their eyes may well be focused on the floor or ceiling.
- **Be specific** – general compliments are not as useful and

185

tend to sound less credible – they can also be countered more easily. For example, compare *'You prepared a brilliant report'* (general) with *'I found the data in that report exceptionally well researched and I appreciated the conciseness of your summary. Well done!'* (specific).

- **Use the person's name.**
- **Be direct and use 'I' statements** – these always have much more impact and are easier to believe (*'I enjoyed your presentation'* rather than *'That was a good presentation'* or *'Your presentation was enjoyable today'*).
- **Be restrained** – avoid using 'over-the-top' adulation, such as *'You're amazing – A miracle – No one could ever live up to your example – How could you not know that you're one in a million?'* In fact, it is probably better to err on the side of understatement until they are able to feel more comfortable with compliment-sharing.
- **Don't include a put-down of yourself** – this is a common fault but is worth trying to eradicate (*'You're such a well-organized person – I only wish I was tidy like you, just look at my desk!'*). A common misconception is that this sort of remark tagged on to a compliment will be an additional boost for people who tend to feel smaller and less capable than most. In reality, all it may achieve is a rise in their anxiety level and reinforcement of their desire to stay at the foot of the pedestal and do something to please and boost you.
- **Don't include an unintentional put-down of them** – because compliment-giving is still a bit embarrassing in our society it is often done in conjunction with light-hearted teasing (*'Well done for ordering that stationery! I was beginning to wonder whether we'd ever see an envelope again in this office!'*). Confident people may not even notice these 'stings in the tail', or they even welcome the challenge to their own wit and humour, but the negative demon within those whose self esteem is low will feed greedily on such remarks. Your compliment will almost certainly have been a waste of breath.
- **Repeat the compliment several times if it is being rejected.** Don't reinforce the low self esteem game of

bouncing appreciation back to the sender.

- **Reinforce your appreciation in writing as often as possible.** Often people with low self esteem find 'black-and-white' compliments much more digestible!
- **Demonstrate the art of taking a compliment well.** For example, you could ask them for a compliment ('*Do you like this colour on me?*'), then demonstrate your pleasure with a broad smile and an appreciative '*Thank you*'. (A particularly pleasant and highly effective way of breaking through resistant defences!)

◇ Exercise – Improving My Compliment-sharing

1. Write down the names of several people whose self esteem could do with an extra boost. Using the above as a guide, note down some compliments you could give them – and set a date for when you are going to do your good deed!
2. Write a short letter or card of appreciation to someone who you think rarely gets one but could perhaps do with one (perhaps some unassuming person who quietly beavers away in an unremarkable corner at your place of work/a distant elderly relative/the station ticket-seller who is particularly welcoming and respectful/someone you have never met but whose suffering you have read about or seen evidence of on TV).

Step 6: Get Some Support for Yourself and Your 'Mission'

In the business of self esteem building, progress can sometimes seem unrewardingly slow. Even though we know that people may be making positive internal psychological changes, when their appearance and behaviour do not immediately reflect this progress it is easy to get discouraged. One of the most important ways of 'insuring' ourselves against potential despondency is to make sure that we ourselves are well supported by people who appreciate what we are trying to do and who understand the process.

There are various ways in which you can provide this support for yourself – for example by:

- regular informal discussions with interested friends
- joining one of the special nationally-organized support networks for people who are committed to building self esteem. These have been established in many countries around the world (details should be readily available through your local health centre, library or mental health association).
- regularly reading books on or listening to programmes about the subject.

At the moment we in Britain are going through a period when this kind of approach to helping people is coming under considerable attack, especially in the sensationalized media. Many people are beginning to panic about the increasing amount of violence and disorder in modern society and are lashing out at us 'do-gooders' with wild unfounded accusations. In this kind of climate even practised hands like myself with years of past successes to bolster us need some ongoing encouragement from 'like minds'. But overall I find the picture extremely encouraging. I know for certain that the interest in personal development is growing fast and furiously.

Building Self Esteem in Others

The greatest revolution of our generation is the discovery that human beings, by changing the inner attitudes of their minds, can change the outer aspects of their lives.

WILLIAM JAMES

So cynics and pessimists beware! During the last 10 years or so the world has begun to amass a formidable army of skilled and knowledgeable self esteem builders who are peacefully but with determination bringing about some staggering psychological changes.

Welcome to the revolution!

Further Reading

John Bradshaw, *Home Coming* (Piatkus, 1991)

Nathaniel Branden, *The Power of Self-Esteem* (Health Communications, 1992)

Philippa Davies, *Personal Power* (Piatkus, 1992)

Deborah M. Hazelton, *Solving the Self-Esteem Puzzle* (Health Communications, 1991)

Judith Lewis Herman, *Trauma and Recovery* (Pandora, 1992)

Jonathon Lazear, *Meditations for Men Who Do Too Much* (Aquarian, 1993)

Gael Lindenfield, *Assert Yourself* (Thorsons, 1986)

—, *Super Confidence* (Thorsons, 1989)

—, *The Positive Woman* (Thorsons, 1992)

—, *Managing Anger* (Thorsons, 1993)

—, *Confident Children* (Thorsons, 1994)

Alan Loy McGinnis, *Bringing Out the Best in People* (Augsburg, 1985)

Matthew McKay and Patrick Fauning, *Self Esteem* (New Harbinger, 1987)

Alice Miller, *The Drama of Being a Child* (Virago, 1987)

Connie D. Palladino, *Developing Self-Esteem* (Kogan Page, 1989)

Vera Pfeiffer, *Positive Thinking* (Element Books, 1989)

Louis Proto, *Take Charge of Your Life* (Thorsons, 1988)

Anthony Robbins, *Unlimited Power* (Simon & Schuster, 1988)

—, *Awaken the Giant Within* (Simon & Schuster, 1992)

John Roger and Peter McWilliams, *You Can't Afford the Luxury of a Negative Thought* (Thorsons, 1991)

Anne Wilson Schaef, *Meditations for Women Who Do Too Much* (HarperSanFrancisco, 1990)

Candice Semigran, *One-Minute Self-Esteem – Caring for Yourself and Others* (Bantam, 1990)

Darlene Deer Truchses, *From Fear to Freedom* (Fulcrum, 1989)

Index